Building a RESTful Web Service with Spring

A hands-on guide to building an enterprise-grade, scalable RESTful web service using the Spring Framework

Ludovic Dewailly

PUBLISHING

BIRMINGHAM - MUMBAI

Building a RESTful Web Service with Spring

First published: October 2015

Production reference: 1081015

Published by Packt Publishing Ltd.
Livery Place
35 Livery Street
Birmingham B3 2PB, UK.

ISBN 978-1-78528-571-4

www.packtpub.com

Credits

Author
Ludovic Dewailly

Reviewers
Fabricio Silva Epaminondas
Greg L. Turnquist

Commissioning Editor
Pratik Shah

Acquisition Editor
Ruchita Bhansali

Content Development Editor
Nikhil Potdukhe

Technical Editor
Menza Mathew

Copy Editor
Angad Singh

Project Coordinator
Izzat Contractor

Proofreader
Safis Editing

Indexer
Rekha Nair

Production Coordinator
Aparna Bhagat

Cover Work
Aparna Bhagat

About the Author

Ludovic Dewailly is a senior, hands-on software engineer and development manager with over 12 years of experience in designing and building software solutions on platforms ranging from resource-constrained mobile devices to cloud-computing systems. He is currently helping FancyGiving.com (a social shopping, wishing, and gifting platform) design and build their system. Ludovic's interests lie in software architecture and tackling the challenges of web scale.

I would like to thank my fiancée, Gaia, for helping me find the time to work on this book, and for dealing with my testiness after late-night writing sessions. I would also like to thank Neil Emerick from NightsBridge (`http://www.nightsbridge.co.za`) for providing me with the idea and concepts behind the sample RESTful web service that outlines this book.

Also, I would like to give gratitude to Chris Laffra and Michael Van Meekeren from the defunct Object Technology International, who gave me my first taste of commercial software development.

Finally, I wish to thank Nikhil Potdukhe and Menza Mathew from Packt Publishing for guiding me and helping me convert the original concept of this project into an actual book.

About the Reviewers

Fabricio Silva Epaminondas has a degree in computer science and a solid background in software development, testing, and engineering. He has been an agile and quality enthusiast for more than 10 years with working experience in the field, having held several roles in fields ranging from project management to software architecture and team leadership.

Fabricio has also worked with mobile, web, and cloud technologies for research institutes and big companies in Brazil and other countries. There, he developed fast and scalable software solutions in the segments of e-commerce, enterprise integration, corporate governance, and innovative solutions.

Fabricio is the technical author of the blog, `fabricioepa.wordpress.com`. You can find out more about his professional profile at `br.linkedin.com/in/fabricioepa`.

> I would like to thank my blessed wife, Buna Suellen, who fully supported me during the production of this book.

Greg L. Turnquist (`@gregturn`) has developed software professionally since 1997. From 2002-2010, he was the lead developer for Harris's $3.5 billion FAA telecommunications program, architecting mission-critical enterprise apps while managing a software team.

In 2010, he joined the Spring team that is now a key part of the start-up company, Pivotal. As a test-bitten script junky, Spring Pro, and JavaScript padawan, Greg works on the Spring Data team while also running the Nashville JUG.

In 2014, he wrote his most recent technical book, *Learning Spring Boot*, for Packt Publishing. He is passionate about application development, writing (fiction and non-fiction), and coffee.

You can read his blog at `http://blog.GregLTurnquist.com`, and also sign up for his newsletter.

www.PacktPub.com

Support files, eBooks, discount offers, and more

For support files and downloads related to your book, please visit www.PacktPub.com.

Did you know that Packt offers eBook versions of every book published, with PDF and ePub files available? You can upgrade to the eBook version at www.PacktPub.com and as a print book customer, you are entitled to a discount on the eBook copy. Get in touch with us at service@packtpub.com for more details.

At www.PacktPub.com, you can also read a collection of free technical articles, sign up for a range of free newsletters and receive exclusive discounts and offers on Packt books and eBooks.

https://www2.packtpub.com/books/subscription/packtlib

Do you need instant solutions to your IT questions? PacktLib is Packt's online digital book library. Here, you can search, access, and read Packt's entire library of books.

Why subscribe?
- Fully searchable across every book published by Packt
- Copy and paste, print, and bookmark content
- On demand and accessible via a web browser

Free access for Packt account holders

If you have an account with Packt at www.PacktPub.com, you can use this to access PacktLib today and view 9 entirely free books. Simply use your login credentials for immediate access.

Table of Contents

Preface

In today's connected world, APIs have taken a central role on the Web. They provide the fabric on which systems interact with each other. And REST has become synonymous with APIs. REpresentational State Transfer, or REST, is an architectural style that lends itself well to tackling the challenges of building scalable web services.

In the Java ecosystem, the Spring Framework is the application framework of choice. It provides a comprehensive programming and configuration model that takes away the "plumbing" of enterprise applications.

It will, therefore, come as no surprise that Spring provides an ideal framework for building RESTful web services. In this book, we will take a hands-on look at how to build an enterprise-grade RESTful web service with the Spring Framework. As an underlying theme, we will illustrate the concepts in each chapter with the implementation of a sample web service that deals with managing rooms in a hotel.

By the end of this book, readers will be equipped with the necessary techniques to create a RESTful web service and sufficient knowledge to scale and secure their web service to meet production readiness requirements.

What this book covers

Chapter 1, A Few Basics, discusses the REST architecture approach and its underlying principles.

Chapter 2, Let's Get Started, enables us to put the scaffolding together, before building a RESTful web service.

Chapter 3, Building RESTful Web Services with Maven and Gradle, looks at the building blocks of creating RESTful endpoints.

Chapter 4, Data Representation, discusses how to manage data representation before we proceed further with building more endpoints. This chapter also offers advice on creating common response formats and error handling.

Chapter 5, CRUD Operations in REST, expands on the previous chapters and takes a look at how you can map CRUD operations to RESTful endpoints.

Chapter 6, Performance, explains that for a web service to be production-ready, it needs to be performant. This chapter discusses performance optimization techniques.

Chapter 7, Dealing with Security, looks at how to ensure a web service is secure by delving into steps that designers need to take. This chapter looks at how to deal with authentication and authorization, as well as input validation techniques.

Chapter 8, Testing Restful Web Services, looks at how to guarantee that a web service delivers the expected functionality, and the testing strategies that designers need to consider. This chapter offers readers the approaches for creating comprehensive test plans.

Chapter 9, Building a REST Client, tells us how for a web service to be of any use, it must be consumed. This penultimate chapter focuses on how to build a client for RESTful web services.

Chapter 10, Scaling a Restful Web Service, explains that scalability is a vast topic and encompasses many aspects. In this last chapter, we discuss what API designers can put in place to help the scaling of their service.

What you need for this book

Readers will need the version 8 of the Java Development Kit (JDK) and Apache Maven to build the code samples in this book. In addition, readers who wish to delve into creating their own service, or simply look at the code samples in more detail, should equip themselves with their preferred IDE.

Who this book is for

This book is intended for those who want to learn to create RESTful web services with the Spring Framework. It goes beyond the use of Spring and explores approaches to tackling resilience, security, and scalability concerns that will prove useful to any service designer. To make the best use of the code samples included in this book, readers should have basic knowledge of the Java language. Any previous experience with the Spring Framework would also help in getting up and running quickly.

Conventions

In this book, you will find a number of text styles that distinguish between different kinds of information. Here are some examples of these styles and an explanation of their meaning.

Code words in text, database table names, folder names, filenames, file extensions, pathnames, dummy URLs, user input, and Twitter handles are shown as follows: "We can include other contexts through the use of the `include` directive."

A block of code is set as follows:

```
import org.springframework.web.bind.annotation.*;

@RestController
public class HelloWorldResource {

    @RequestMapping(method = RequestMethod.GET)
    public String helloWorld() {
        return "Hello, world!";
    }
}
```

When we wish to draw your attention to a particular part of a code block, the relevant lines or items are set in bold:

```
<dependency>
  <groupId>com.packtpub.rest-with-spring</groupId>
  <artifactId>rest-with-spring-billing</artifactId>
  <version>1.0.0-SNAPSHOT</version>
  <classifier>classes</classifier>
</dependency>
```

Any command-line input or output is written as follows:

```
mvn jetty:start
```

New terms and **important words** are shown in bold. Words that you see on the screen, for example, in menus or dialog boxes, appear in the text like this: "For example, with **IntelliJ IDEA**, our sample web service project can be imported by selecting the menu options **File | Open**."

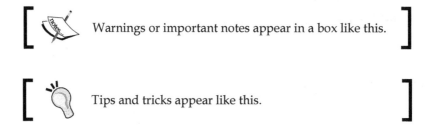

Warnings or important notes appear in a box like this.

Tips and tricks appear like this.

Reader feedback

Feedback from our readers is always welcome. Let us know what you think about this book—what you liked or disliked. Reader feedback is important for us as it helps us develop titles that you will really get the most out of.

To send us general feedback, simply e-mail feedback@packtpub.com, and mention the book's title in the subject of your message.

If there is a topic that you have expertise in and you are interested in either writing or contributing to a book, see our author guide at www.packtpub.com/authors.

Customer support

Now that you are the proud owner of a Packt book, we have a number of things to help you to get the most from your purchase.

Downloading the example code

You can download the example code files from your account at http://www.packtpub.com for all the Packt Publishing books you have purchased. If you purchased this book elsewhere, you can visit http://www.packtpub.com/support and register to have the files e-mailed directly to you.

Errata

Although we have taken every care to ensure the accuracy of our content, mistakes do happen. If you find a mistake in one of our books—maybe a mistake in the text or the code—we would be grateful if you could report this to us. By doing so, you can save other readers from frustration and help us improve subsequent versions of this book. If you find any errata, please report them by visiting http://www.packtpub.com/submit-errata, selecting your book, clicking on the **Errata Submission Form** link, and entering the details of your errata. Once your errata are verified, your submission will be accepted and the errata will be uploaded to our website or added to any list of existing errata under the Errata section of that title.

To view the previously submitted errata, go to https://www.packtpub.com/books/content/support and enter the name of the book in the search field. The required information will appear under the **Errata** section.

Piracy

Piracy of copyrighted material on the Internet is an ongoing problem across all media. At Packt, we take the protection of our copyright and licenses very seriously. If you come across any illegal copies of our works in any form on the Internet, please provide us with the location address or website name immediately so that we can pursue a remedy.

Please contact us at copyright@packtpub.com with a link to the suspected pirated material.

We appreciate your help in protecting our authors and our ability to bring you valuable content.

Questions

If you have a problem with any aspect of this book, you can contact us at questions@packtpub.com, and we will do our best to address the problem.

1
A Few Basics

With the prominence of the Internet and the ubiquity of **HTTP** in today's world, **web services** have become the main means for web-based systems to interoperate with each other. A web service is an interface that provides access to a web-facing system for clients and other services to consume.

Simple Object Access Protocol (SOAP) used to be the de facto choice for building such services. SOAP is an **XML**-based communication protocol, leveraging open standards. However, in recent years **Representational State Transfer** (**REST**) has become a very popular alternative to traditional SOAP web services. So, let's take a look at the principles behind REST. This chapter will cover the following topics:

- Discussions of the REST principles
- How the Spring Framework can help in the building of **RESTful** web services
- A sample RESTful web service that will provide the backdrop for the rest of this book

REST principles

REST is a software architecture approach for creating scalable web services. The term **REST** was coined by Roy Fielding in his PhD dissertation, and revolves around a number of principles. These principles underpin the architecture of RESTful web services and are described in the following sections.

Uniform interface

At the core of REST are resources, and resources are identified using **Uniform Resource Identifiers** (**URIs**). Conceptually, resources are separate from their representation (that is, the format in which they are provided to clients). REST does not mandate any specific format, but typically includes **XML** and **JSON** (which will be discussed in *Chapter 4, Data Representation*).

In addition, resource representations are self-descriptive. In more concrete terms, this means that sufficient information must be returned for the successful processing of responses.

Another distinctive property of REST is that clients interact entirely through hypermedia, which is dynamically provided by the application servers. Apart from endpoints, clients need no prior knowledge of how to interact with a RESTful service. This constraint is referred to as **Hypermedia as the Engine of Application State** (**HATEOAS**).

Client-Server

The client-server model that REST embraces enables the separation of client concerns, such as user interaction or user state management, from that of server concerns such as data storage and scalability.

This decoupling ensures that, provided an interface that is agreed upon, the development of client and server can be done independently. It also helps reduce complexity and improve the effectiveness of performance tuning.

Stateless

REST advocates statelessness. No client state is stored on the server. All the information needed to perform operations is contained in the requests (as part of the URL, request body, or as HTTP headers).

Cacheable

RESTful web services must provide caching capabilities. Servers can indicate how and for how long to cache responses. Clients can use cached responses instead of contacting the server.

 This principle has significant advantages for scalability. Caching techniques will be discussed in *Chapter 6, Performance*.

Since REST typically leverages HTTP, it inherits all the caching properties that HTTP offers.

Layered system

Given the style of communication between clients and servers, clients are not aware of which specific server they are interacting with. This property allows the introduction of intermediate servers that can, for example, handle security or offer load-balancing capabilities. These architectural concepts are discussed in more detail in *Chapter 10, Scaling a RESTful Web Service*.

Code on demand

Even though it's part of the REST architecture, this principal is optional. Servers can temporarily extend the functionality of clients by transferring executable code. For example, JavaScript can be provided to web-based clients to customize functionality.

For a service to be considered RESTful, it should abide by the preceding principles.

The Spring Framework and REST

It is assumed that the reader is familiar with the **Spring Framework** (referred to as **Spring** from here on). We will therefore focus on the specificities of building RESTful web services with Spring, in this section.

Since REST hinges on URIs, the Spring Web MVC framework provides all the necessary tools for building RESTful endpoints. Annotations, such as `org.springframework.web.bind.annotation.RequestMapping` and `org.springframework.web.bind.annotation.RequestParam` for mapping URLs and parameters form the basis for creating such endpoints. *Chapter 3, The First Endpoint*, will discuss these annotations and offer code samples to illustrate their use.

 Reference documentation about the Spring Web MVC can be found at `http://docs.spring.io/spring/docs/current/spring-framework-reference/html/mvc.html`.

With the technological context laid out, let's now look at one such RESTful service. Throughout this book, we will be building a sample web service that helps manage hotels and B&Bs.

Our RESTful web service

One common piece of software in use in the hospitality industry is a property management system (careful readers will notice the unfortunate acronym for these systems). It allows automating the operations of hotels and B&Bs. For the purpose of this book, we will build such a system using Spring. Each component of this system will expose a RESTful **API** that will be consumed by a simple web interface.

 Designing effective Application Programming Interfaces is a topic that deserves its own treaty. It is beyond the scope of this book to discuss these concerns in detail. The main characteristics that one should bear in mind when designing APIs are: ease of use, consistency, exposing as little as necessary, extensibility, and forward compatibility.

Architecture

Our property management system will be formed of the four components, as illustrated in the following figure:

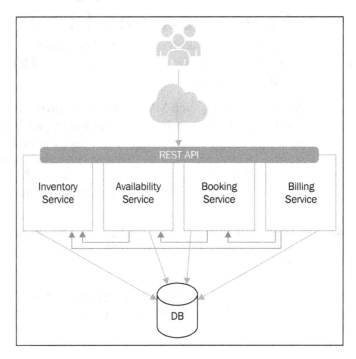

The four components are explained as follows:

- **Inventory Service**: This component provides the necessary functionality to manage and describe rooms and room types.

- **Availability Service**: This component lets users see what rooms are available on specific dates.

- **Booking Service**: This component will be responsible for taking bookings. It will rely on the Inventory Service and Availability Service components to validate bookings.

- **Billing Service**: Once a booking is made, this component will offer the ability to generate an invoice.

Data model

In this section, we will look at the data model that will support our web service. The following entity relationship diagram provides an overview of this model:

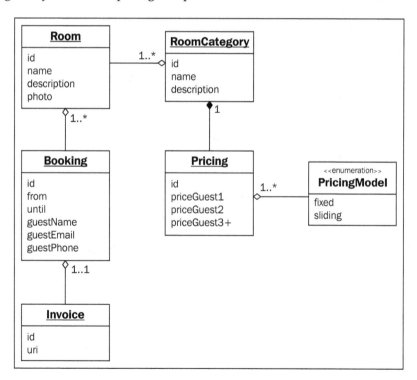

The entities that constitute our model are as follows:

- **Room**: This object represents the physical rooms that are part of our hotel. Rooms have a name and a description as well as photos.
- **RoomCategory**: Each room belongs to a category (for example, double room). Categories provide a description, and are linked to a pricing model.
- **Pricing**: This object encapsulates how rooms are priced (for example, a fixed price, or a sliding price based on the number of guests).
- **Booking**: The reservation of rooms is modeled on bookings. Bookings will capture the reserved room, dates, and contact details for guests.
- **Invoice**: This provides invoices to guests upon booking. They contain the relevant information regarding the booking, and the amount to be settled.

The data access layer will be implemented using **Object-Relational Mapping (ORM)** with Hibernate 4.3.8.

> We will not delve into the specificities of Hibernate ORM in this book. However, documentation is available on Hibernate.org at `http://hibernate.org/orm/`.

In addition, for the purpose of simplifying the development and testing of our web service, we will use an embedded H2 database.

> Documentation about H2 can be found at `http://www.h2database.com`.

Hibernate supports H2 out of the box, so no specific setup is required to use it as our embedded database.

> While an embedded database is great for development, it is not fit for a production deployment.

Summary

Now that we had a look at the topics that we will cover in this book, and what our RESTful web service will do, let's discuss how we are going to build it.

In the next chapter, we will see the description of several tools available to help us create our sample web service.

2
Building RESTful Web Services with Maven and Gradle

As mentioned in the previous chapter, we will build a sample property management system as a RESTful web service. Before we dig into the implementation, let's first take a look at how the service will be put together. In this chapter, we will discuss the following topics:

- Building a RESTful web service with **Apache Maven**
- Building a RESTful web service with **Gradle**
- Structuring our property management web service
- Running and debugging a Spring-based web service

Apache Maven

Maven is an open-source software project management tool. It was born out of the need to simplify Ant-based builds and it favors convention over configuration. In more concrete terms, it offers out of the box support for typical workflows, such as building Java web applications, provided one follows its conventions. However, customizing the build process can prove challenging, and many of its detractors point this design choice out as the main motivation for not using Maven.

 More information on Maven can be found at
https://maven.apache.org.

While Maven offers many features, they are beyond the scope of this chapter. We will focus on its support for building Java web applications.

The following **POM (Project Object Model)** file illustrates how a project can be declared with Maven (in a file called *pom.xml*):

```
<project xmlns="http://maven.apache.org/POM/4.0.0" xmlns:xsi="http://
www.w3.org/2001/XMLSchema-instance"
    xsi:schemaLocation="http://maven.apache.org/POM/4.0.0 http://
maven.apache.org/xsd/maven-4.0.0.xsd">
    <modelVersion>4.0.0</modelVersion>

    <groupId>com.packtpub.rest-with-spring</groupId>
    <artifactId>rest-with-spring</artifactId>
    <version>1.0.0-SNAPSHOT</version>
    <packaging>war</packaging>

</project>
```

This pom.xml file defines a project with a group identifier, artifact identifier, and version. It also describes how the resulting application will be packaged (as a WAR file in this case).

 Maven artifacts belong to a group (typically com.company.application), and must have a unique identifier (typically the application's name).

Developers are free to choose their versioning schemes. However, Maven works best with a version of the form x.y, where x is the major version number and y the minor version number.

 The SNAPSHOT version suffix tells Maven that this project is currently in development. It has implications for the way artifacts are handled by the dependency resolution, as explained in the following section.

Dependency management in Apache Maven

One build feature that makes development much easier is dependency management. It alleviates the need to manually download third-party libraries and package them with the application. Maven has robust dependency management based on artifact repositories.

The main repository for Maven is called the Central Repository and can be searched on at http://maven.org.

To declare dependencies, the sample POM file that was presented in the previous section can be amended in the following fashion:

```
// content omitted for readability purposes
    <version>1.0.0-SNAPSHOT</version>
    <packaging>war</packaging>
    <dependencies>
        <dependency>
            <groupId>org.hibernate</groupId>
            <artifactId>hibernate-core</artifactId>
            <version>4.1.9.Final</version>
        </dependency>
        <!-- Test Dependencies -->
        <dependency>
            <groupId>junit</groupId>
            <artifactId>junit</artifactId>
            <version>4.11</version>
            <scope>test</scope>
        </dependency>
    </dependencies>
</project>
```

The `<dependencies>` element in the amended POM file declares two dependencies:

- **Hibernate**: This is a standard dependency that Maven will automatically fetch before compiling the project
- **JUnit**: With this dependency, Maven will alter the classpath used to compile and execute the unit tests

Another build tool that has gathered a lot of popularity is Gradle and it is discussed in the next section

Gradle

Gradle is a project automation tool that borrows a lot of concepts from Maven. It differs from Maven in using a **Groovy**-based declarative syntax instead of **XML**.

 Read more about Gradle at https://gradle.org. And, head over to http://www.groovy-lang.org for an introduction to Groovy.

Gradle has become a popular alternative to Maven for its flexibility and neater declarative syntax, while still offering powerful dependency management. We will take a quick look at dependency management in the next section.

Dependency management in Gradle

Gradle offers dependency resolution. It can be set up to use Maven's Central Repository. Let's consider a sample Gradle build (in a file called `build.gradle`):

```
apply plugin: 'java'

repositories {
    mavenCentral()
}
```

We instructed Gradle that we want to build a Java project and that the dependencies should be fetched from Maven's Central Repository. Now, we can simply declare the dependencies we require as follows:

```
dependencies {
  runtime group: 'org.hibernate', name: 'hibernate-core',
    version: '4.1.9.Final'
  testCompile group: 'junit', name: 'junit', version: '4.+'
}
```

The following Gradle build file declares two dependencies:

- **Hibernate**: This is a runtime dependency that will be used during the project compilation and will be packaged with the application
- **JUnit**: This dependency is added to the classpath that is used while running the tests. This type of dependency does not get included in the final application

It is possible to use a remote Maven repository by adding the following to the build file:

```
repositories {
    maven {
        url "http://repo.mycompany.com"
    }
}
```

Maven and Gradle both offer excellent support for building our sample RESTful service, and the full build scripts can be downloaded along with all the source code of this book. Now, let's turn our attention to the structure of our property management system.

The structure of our sample web service

In *Chapter 1, A Few Basics*, we decomposed this application into four components:

- Inventory Service
- Availability Service
- Booking Service
- Billing Service

One approach would be to build our project as a single module and have the code of these four services together.

While it makes the setup quite straightforward, it might impede our ability to deploy these components individually, should it be required for scalability purposes (refer to *Chapter 10, Scaling a RESTful Web Service*, for discussions on scalability). Instead, we will organize each service into its own individual module.

For the purpose of this section, we will focus on Maven. Our project will be made up of six separate Maven modules:

- common: This module contains common code and the Hibernate setup that is to be used
- inventory: This is the inventory service implementation
- availability: This is the availability service implementation
- booking: This is the booking service implementation
- billing: This is the billing service implementation

- `all`: This is a module that constructs a single web application using the four services for development and single deployment purposes

 Refer to the documents found at `https://maven.apache.org/guides/mini/guide-multiple-modules.html` for more information on working with Maven modules.

Our parent POM file will therefore look like this:

```
<project ... // omitted for readability
    <modelVersion>4.0.0</modelVersion>

    <groupId>com.packtpub.rest-with-spring</groupId>
    <artifactId>rest-with-spring</artifactId>
    <version>1.0.0-SNAPSHOT</version>
    <packaging>pom</packaging>

    <modules>
        <module>common</module>
        <module>inventory</module>
        <module>availability</module>
        <module>booking</module>
        <module>billing</module>
        <module>all</module>
    </modules>

</project>
```

As listed previously, our modules are declared in this top-level *pom.xml*. The `common` module is a simple JAR module, whereas `inventory`, `availability`, `booking`, `billing`, and `all` are declared as WAR modules.

 The complete Maven setup can be downloaded **TODO**.

The anatomy of a Service Module

With the overall project structure defined, we can now focus on how each module (for example, `booking`) is declared.

Some of the service modules have runtime dependencies on other services modules. For instance, `billing` relies on the booking service defined in `booking`.

Out of the box, Maven provides support for packaging a module as a **WAR (Web Application Archive)**. However, it doesn't expose the Java code as an artifact. To do so, our service modules must contain the following configuration:

```
<project>
    <modelVersion>4.0.0</modelVersion>

    <parent>
        <groupId>com.packtpub.rest-with-spring</groupId>
        <artifactId>rest-with-spring</artifactId>
        <version>1.0.0-SNAPSHOT</version>
    </parent>

    <artifactId>rest-with-spring-billing</artifactId>
    <packaging>war</packaging>

    <build>
        <plugins>
            <plugin>
                <artifactId>maven-war-plugin</artifactId>
                <version>2.6</version>
                <configuration>
                    <attachClasses>true</attachClasses>
                </configuration>
            </plugin>
        </plugins>
    </build>
</project>
```

The plugin responsible for building the WAR file is instructed to attach the Java code as a separate artifact that can then be referenced elsewhere. The snippet that follows illustrates how to reference this artifact:

```
<dependency>
    <groupId>com.packtpub.rest-with-spring</groupId>
    <artifactId>rest-with-spring-billing</artifactId>
    <version>1.0.0-SNAPSHOT</version>
    <classifier>classes</classifier>
</dependency>
```

This is a fairly standard dependency declaration except for the `classifier` element, which refers to the Java code for the service.

Local versus Remote Service Invocations

At this point, you may be wondering how, if each service is deployed separately, they will call each other.

In the context of a single deployment, these invocations would be simple Java calls. However, in a distributed system, the RESTful API will be leveraged.

To make the code agnostic of the mode of operation, we will declare our services as interfaces, and with Spring, either inject the actual implementation in a single deployment mode, or inject a client implementation (*Chapter 9*, *Building a REST Client*, discusses how to build service clients) in a distributed mode of operation.

Developing RESTful web services

In this section, we will provide a few tips to effectively develop Spring-based RESTful web services.

Working with your favorite IDE

Maven and Gradle are well-supported tools and most integrated development environments, or **IDEs**, provide a way to import such projects. For example, with **IntelliJ IDEA**, our sample web service project can be imported by selecting the menu options **File | Open**. Once imported, the project will be shown as follows:

With the project imported, we can start implementing our property management system web service. Before we do so, however, let's discuss how to execute our service.

 Both Eclipse and NetBeans also offer support for Maven and Gradle (via plugins).

Making services executable

With Maven or Gradle, it is possible to package the service in a WAR format. However, to quickly start and debug the application during development, we are going to implement an executable Java class. With **Spring Boot** it is easily achieved via the following class:

```
package com.packtpub.restspring.app;

import org.springframework.boot.SpringApplication;
import org.springframework.boot.autoconfigure.SpringBootApplication;

@SpringBootApplication
public class WebApplication {

    public static void main(String[] args) {
        SpringApplication.run(WebApplication.class, args);
    }
}
```

This class bootstraps our application by discovering all the web components and loading them.

 Add the following Maven dependency to access `org.springframework.boot.SpringApplication`:
```
<dependency>
    <groupId>org.springframework.boot</groupId>
    <artifactId>spring-boot-starter-web</artifactId>
    <version>1.2.3.RELEASE</version>
</dependency>
```

The good thing about Spring Boot is that it requires no setup or configuration. Once this class is executed, the service will be available on port 8080 via an embedded Tomcat server.

 Information on Spring Boot can be found at `http://projects.spring.io/spring-boot/`

Starting services with Maven

Another approach to start a web service (without an IDE) during development is by using the Jetty Maven plugin. The following POM extract illustrates the necessary configuration:

```
<build>
  <plugins>
    ...
    <plugin>
      <groupId>org.mortbay.jetty</groupId>
      <artifactId>jetty-maven-plugin</artifactId>
      <configuration>
        <useTestScope>true</useTestScope>
        <stopPort>8005</stopPort>
        <stopKey>DIE!</stopKey>
        <systemProperties>
          <systemProperty>
            <name>jetty.port</name>
            <value>8080</value>
          </systemProperty>
        </systemProperties>
      </configuration>
    </plugin>
  </plugins>
</build>
```

With this plugin element added to the POM file, it is now possible to start the service by running the following command:

`mvn jetty:start`

The service will then be available at `http://localhost:8080`.

Note that while the service is running, the application does not expose any endpoints. The next chapter will look at how to create RESTful endpoints, but for now, developers can create the following controller to quickly test the service:

```
import org.springframework.web.bind.annotation.*;

@RestController
public class HelloWorldResource {

    @RequestMapping(method = RequestMethod.GET)
    public String helloWorld() {
        return "Hello, world!";
    }
}
```

With this controller in place, invoking `http://localhost:8080` will display the following:

```
Hello, world!
```

Summary

We saw how to set up a Maven or Gradle build to support the implementation of a RESTful web service. It is now time to start implementing our sample web service. The next chapter will introduce the first REST endpoint.

3

The First Endpoint

In the previous chapter, we looked at how to set up the scaffolding required to build a RESTful web service. We can now start implementing our first endpoint. As introduced in *Chapter 1, A Few Basics*, Spring Web MVC provides the necessary tools to create controllers in a RESTful manner. To illustrate their use, we will lean on our sample web service. More specifically, we will start implementing the Inventory component of our service.

This chapter will go over the following topics:

- The Inventory component of our sample web service
- Spring constructs to build RESTful endpoints
- Running our first endpoint
- A brief discussion on data presentation

The Inventory service

At the heart of our property management service lies rooms that are the representations of physical rooms that guests can reserve. They are organized in categories. A room category is a logical grouping of similar rooms. For example, we could have a *Double Rooms* category for all rooms with double beds. Rooms exhibit properties as per the code snippet that follows:

```
@Entity(name = "rooms")
public class Room {

    private long id;
    private RoomCategory roomCategory;
    private String name;
    private String description;
```

```
@Id
@GeneratedValue
public long getId() {
  return id;
}

@ManyToOne(cascade = {CascadeType.PERSIST,
  CascadeType.REFRESH}, fetch = FetchType.EAGER)
public RoomCategory getRoomCategory() {
  return roomCategory;
}

@Column(name = "name", unique = true, nullable = false,
  length = 128)
public String getName() {
  return name;
}

@Column(name = "description")
public String getDescription() {
  return description;
}
}
```

With the use of the **Java Persistence API (JPA)** and Hibernate, rooms have an auto-generated identifier (thanks to the @javax.persistence.Id and @javax.persistence.GeneratedValue annotations): a unique and mandatory name along with an optional description.

 JPA is not in the scope of this book. Information on it can be found at http://en.wikipedia.org/wiki/Java_Persistence_API

Additionally, a one-to-many relationship is established between categories and rooms with the use of the @javax.persistence.ManyToOne annotation.

The Inventory service provides access to rooms and their categories. Several operations are made available by this component. However, we are only interested in one of the operations in this chapter. Therefore, let's consider the following Java interface:

```
public interface InventoryService {

  public Room getRoom(long roomId);

  // other methods omitted for clarity
}
```

This service interface gives us the ability to look up a room by its identifier. Assuming that we have an implementation for this interface, the next step is to expose this operation through our RESTful interface. The following section describes how to go about doing just that.

REST and the MVC pattern

The Spring Web MVC module provides an implementation of the traditional **Model View Controller** pattern. While REST does not mandate the use of any specific pattern, using the MVC pattern is quite a natural fit whereby the RESTful resource or model is exposed through a controller. The view in our case will be a JSON representation of the model.

Without further ado, let's take a look at our first endpoint:

```
@RestController
@RequestMapping("/rooms")
public class RoomsResource {

  private final InventoryService inventoryService;

  public RoomsResource(InventoryService inventoryService) {
    this.inventoryService = inventoryService;
  }

  @RequestMapping(value = "/{roomId}", method = RequestMethod.GET)
  public RoomDTO getRoom(@PathVariable("roomId") String roomId) {
    RoomDTO room = ...
    // omitted for sake of clarity
    return room;
  }
}
```

With the use of `@org.springframework.web.bind.annotation.RestController`, we instruct Spring that `RoomsResource` is a controller.

 Traditionally, one would expect this controller class to be called `RoomController`. However, in the RESTful architectural style, the core concept revolves around resources. Therefore, using the *Resource* suffix embodies the REST principles more appropriately.

The other annotation of note in this code is `@org.springframework.web.bind.annotation.RequestMapping`. This is discussed in the next section.

 The **Data Transfer Object (DTO)** pattern is referenced here (RoomDTO), but we will look at it in more detail in *Chapter 4, Data Representation*. It provides a useful decoupling between the persistence and presentation layers.

Request mapping

The `@org.springframework.web.bind.annotation.RequestMapping` annotation provides the glue for mapping incoming requests to classes and methods within the code.

Path mapping

Typically, at the class level, the `@org.springframework.web.bind.annotation.RequestMapping` annotation allows routing requests for a specific path to a resource (or controller) class. For example, in the previous code extract, the `RoomsResource` class declares the top-level request mapping, `@RequestMapping("/rooms")`. With this annotation, the class will handle all requests to the path, `rooms`.

HTTP method mapping

It is possible to map specific HTTP methods to classes or Java methods. Our `RoomsResource` class exposes a method for retrieving a `Room` by identifier. It is declared as follows:

```
@RequestMapping(value = "/{roomId}", method = RequestMethod.GET)
```

In combination with the class-level annotation, `GET` requests with the following `/rooms/{roomId}` value will be mapped to `RoomsResource.getRoom()`.

Requests with any other methods (say, `PUT` or `DELETE`) will not be mapped to this Java method.

Request parameter mapping

Besides path parameters, request parameters can also be referenced in a
RestController class. The @org.springframework.web.bind.annotation.
RequestParam parameter provides the means to map an HTTP query parameter
to a Java method attribute. To illustrate parameter mapping, let's add a new lookup
method to our resource:

```
@RequestMapping(method = RequestMethod.GET)
public List<RoomDTO> getRoomsInCategory(@RequestParam(
  "categoryId") long categoryId) {
  RoomCategory category = inventoryService.getRoomCategory(
    categoryId);
  return inventoryService.getAllRoomsWithCategory(category)
  .stream().map(RoomDTO::new).collect(Collectors.toList());
}
```

Requests to URLs, such as http://localhost:8080/rooms?categoryId=1, will
be handled by this method, and the categoryId method attribute will be set to 1.
The method will return a list of rooms for the given category in the JSON format,
as follows:

```
[
  {
    "id": 1,
    "name": "Room 1",
    "roomCategoryId": 1,
    "description": "Nice, spacious double bed room with usual
      amenities"
  }
]
```

Service designers could also declare this endpoint without using
a parameter. For example, the URL pattern could be /rooms/
categories/{categoryId}. This approach has the added
benefit of improving caching, since not all browsers and proxies
cache query parameters. Refer to *Chapter 6, Performance*, for more
details on caching techniques.

As we continue implementing our property management system in the rest of the
book, we will put into practice these mapping constructs. *Chapter 5, CRUD Operations
in REST*, will especially highlight how to map CRUD (Create, Read, Update, and
Delete) operations in REST with these annotations.

The preceding code snippet makes use of Java's new Stream API, which is some functional programming goodness introduced in Java 8. Read more about it at `https://docs.oracle.com/javase/8/docs/api/java/util/stream/Stream.html`.

Running the service

Building upon *Chapter 2, Building RESTful Web Services with Maven and Gradle*, we can quickly get our service up and running by using Spring Boot. For this purpose, we need to create a main class, as follows:

```
package com.packtpub.springrest.inventory;
// imports omitted
@SpringBootApplication
public class WebApplication {

  public static void main(String[] args) {
    SpringApplication.run(new Object[]{WebApplication.class,
      "inventory.xml"}, args);
    InventoryService inventoryService = context.getBean(
      InventoryService.class);
  }
}
```

Running this class in your favorite IDE will start an embedded **Tomcat** instance and expose your resources. The service will be accessible at `http://localhost:8080`. For example, accessing `http://localhost:8080/rooms/1` will return the following:

```
{
  "id": 1,
  "name": "Room 1",
  "roomCategoryId": 1,
  "description": "Nice, spacious double bed room with usual
    amenities"
}
```

We depart from *Chapter 2, Building RESTful Web Services with Maven and Gradle*, in this example by mixing auto detection and XML-based strategies. By passing both the application class and the name of our XML Spring wiring (`inventory.xml`), Spring Boot will load all the annotated beans it can find, along with the ones declared in XML.

A few words on data representation

Without us doing anything, our DTO objects are magically converted to JSON by Spring. This is thanks to Spring's support for data binding with **Jackson**. The Jackson JSON processor provides a fast and lightweight library for mapping Java objects to JSON objects.

Summary

In this chapter, we discussed the `Inventory` component of our sample RESTful web service and worked on our first endpoint. We explored how to quickly run and access this endpoint, and we even threw in a bonus endpoint to list rooms by categories.

In the next chapter, we will explore in more detail how to control the JSON format of responses, along with the DTO pattern and why it is useful for decoupling the different layers of a system.

4
Data Representation

We looked at how to build a RESTful endpoint in the previous chapter. We also briefly discussed how the data is represented in REST responses. In this chapter, we will expand on these discussions and cover the following topics:

- The Data-Transfer-Object design pattern
- Controlling the responses format in JSON
- Tips on formatting responses
- API evolutions

Before we delve into the specifics of how to control our JSON responses, let's first take a look at the DTO design pattern.

The Data-Transfer-Object design pattern

A data transfer object is a simple wrapper around properties, which is passed between layers of an application. This pattern offers a good abstraction level between how the data is stored and managed internally and how it is represented.

Such objects typically define no business logic, and simply fulfill the role of a data container. In the context of our sample property management web service, we declare, for example, a DTO class for Rooms. The following code snippet illustrates this DTO class:

```
public class RoomDTO implements Serializable {

    private static final long serialVersionUID = 2682046985632747474L;

    private long id;
    private String name;
    private long roomCategoryId;
```

```
        private String description;

        public RoomDTO(Room room) {
            this.id = room.getId();
            this.name = room.getName();
            this.roomCategoryId = room.getRoomCategory().getId();
            this.description = room.getDescription();
        }

        public long getId() {
            return id;
        }

        public String getName() {
            return name;
        }

        public long getRoomCategoryId() {
            return roomCategoryId;
        }

        public String getDescription() {
            return description;
        }
    }
```

In this example, we defined the attributes of a room that we wanted to make available to the data layer of our service (in this case, the JSON responses of our API). Our data layer object was passed as a constructor parameter so that the DTO object can be easily initialized.

DTO objects do not need to implement `java.io.Serializable`. It can, however, be useful to do so, in order to run the different layers of an application in separate JVMs.

 You can read further about this pattern on Wikipedia at `http://en.wikipedia.org/wiki/Data_transfer_object`

Readers might also know this pattern as the **Value-Object** design pattern. Early Java EE literature mistakenly used this term to describe the notion of a data transfer object. Semantically, the VO pattern is quite different from the DTO design pattern. Where DTO objects are customized versions of model objects, VO objects represent fixed sets of data, similar to a Java `enum`. They are usually identified by their values and are immutable.

> When using the Java Persistence API (as we did in our sample web service with Hibernate), DTOs become very useful. Mixing persistence and presentation concerns in one class is quite tricky and often leads to clashes.

The API response format

It is up to API designers to decide which format best suits their use case. That being said, it is good practice to settle on a common response envelope format. With this approach, a RESTful web service provides a uniform interface, enabling the client developers to handle responses in a consistent manner, regardless of the operation being invoked.

The next section offers a sample envelope format.

The envelope format

The first piece of information that is relevant to any operation is whether it was successful. We can encapsulate that information with a status. Secondly, most requests will return data. Therefore, a field in our envelope could provide generic access to the response payload. The following format will form the base of any responses returned by the API:

```
{
    "status": "OK",
    "data": {...}
}
```

With this response format, we ensured that client developers will have a consistent way to check if a request was successful and access the payload.

Error management

Knowing that a request failed is important, but on the face of it, not very useful. Ideally, we should provide some details about why the request failed. For example, a request could have an invalid parameter value, or the requester may not be authorized to perform the operation.

Error handling is an important aspect of designing a robust and well-documented API. Since most RESTful web services are accessed over HTTP/HTTPS, we can leverage HTTP status codes to categorize errors and provide clues as to what is wrong with a request.

> For example, servers should return a 403 HTTP error code if an operation is not permitted, or a 400 HTTP error code if a request parameter is invalid.

Beyond HTTP response codes, API developers may wish to provide their own error codes in responses to provide service consumers with more clues about why an operation is failing. To facilitate this, we can modify our suggested envelope format to include an error property:

```
{
  "status": "ERROR",
  "data": null,
  "error": {
    "errorCode": 999,
    "description": "Email address is invalid"
  }
}
```

In this example, the operation could not be successfully completed because an invalid e-mail address was passed. Our response contained an error property specifying an application-specific error code and description.

Pagination support

For operations returning a list of resources to be scalable, they must provide some form of pagination. In our sample web service, for instance, we provide an endpoint, listing all the rooms in a given category, as described in *Chapter 3, The First Endpoint*. We could therefore extend our suggested envelope format to include pagination information in this situation. Let's consider the following JSON response:

```
{
  "status": "OK",
  "data": [...],
```

```
    "error": null,
    "pageNumber": 1,
    "nextPage": "http://localhost:8080/rooms?categoryId=1&page=2",
    "total": 13
}
```

In addition to the standard properties, we include the page number returned along with the total number of resources available, and a reference to the next page of resources.

Customizing JSON responses

To adhere to guidelines or requirements, API designers may want to control how JSON responses are formatted. As mentioned in *Chapter 3*, *The First Endpoint*, Spring Web makes use of Jackson to perform JSON serialization. Therefore, to customize our JSON format, we must configure the Jackson processor. Spring Web offers XML-based or Java-based approaches to handling configuration. In the following, we will look at the Java-based configuration.

Let's pretend that we are required to have property names in lower case with underscore, instead of camel case. In order to reduce the size of responses, we are also asked not to include properties with null values.

By default, responses are formatted as follows:

```
{
    "status": "OK",
    "data": {
    "id": 1,
    "name": "Room 1",
    "roomCategoryId": 1,
    "description": "Nice, spacious double bed room with usual
amenities"
    },
    "error": null
}
```

If we create a WebMvcConfigurerAdapter extension, then we are provided with the ability to instruct Jackson on how to format JSON messages:

```
@Configuration
@EnableWebMvc
public class JsonConfiguration extends WebMvcConfigurerAdapter {

    @Override
```

```
public void configureMessageConverters(
  List<HttpMessageConverter<?>> converters) {
  converters.add(new MappingJackson2HttpMessageConverter(
    new Jackson2ObjectMapperBuilder()
  .propertyNamingStrategy(PropertyNamingStrategy.
    CAMEL_CASE_TO_LOWER_CASE_WITH_UNDERSCORES)
  .serializationInclusion(Include.NON_NULL)
  .build()));
  }
}
```

When the application is started, Spring will discover this class (thanks to the @Configuration annotation), and add our converter, MappingJackson2HttpMessageConverter. We configure this converter to format property names in lower case with underscore, as well as tell Jackson to ignore null properties. The resulting JSON format will be as follows:

```
{
  "status": "OK",
  "data": {
    "id": 1,
    "name": "Room 1",
    "room_category_id": 1,
    "description": "Nice, spacious double bed room with usual
      amenities"
  }
}
```

We can see that the error property is now gone, and the room category ID property name is in the format we were asked to use.

> org.springframework.http.converter.json.
> Jackson2ObjectMapperBuilder offers many more options
> to control the JSON format. The Javadoc is available at http://
> docs.spring.io/spring/docs/current/javadoc-
> api/org/springframework/http/converter/json/
> Jackson2ObjectMapperBuilder.html

This section has given the reader the basic tools to control the formatting of responses. These response formats should be considered parts of the service API, and therefore modifications to existing responses should be managed with care. The next section discusses how such concerns can be managed with versioning.

API evolutions

Systems evolve over time, and the functionality that they expose changes along with these evolutions. APIs, be it in the form of a library or a RESTful API, must adapt to these changes while maintaining some form of backward compatibility.

It is therefore a good idea to consider evolutions when designing APIs. The next section describes how **HATEOAS (Hypermedia As The Engine Of Application State)** can be leveraged to manage evolutions.

HATEOAS

This REST principle provides a method for self-discovery for service consumers. Let's consider the following response to a RESTful endpoint:

```
{
  "id": 1,
  "category": "http://myservice.com/categories/33",
  ...
}
```

This response includes a hypermedia link to a related resource, so consumers do not need prior knowledge of where to fetch the resource from.

With this approach, service designers can manage evolutions by introducing new hypermedia links as changes occur, and retiring old links without requiring service consumers to be modified. It is a powerful mechanism that can help effectively manage service evolutions.

Versioning strategies

While the purists will disagree with the use of versioning in RESTful web services, in real world situations, versioning provides a useful mechanism to manage major evolutions of an API. With resources being at the center of REST, a natural place for versioning is in the URI.

URI versioning

Let's consider the following URI `/rooms/{roomId}` that provides access to a room resource, as described in *The Data-Transfer-Object design pattern* section. We want to add a new field containing a URL pertaining to a picture of the room (`pictureUrl`). Such a change is forward-compatible and does not require specific treatment for clients to continue consuming the service.

Now, we realize that having more than one picture would improve user engagement. We could simply add a new field along with the existing picture URL. However, it makes more sense to just replace the picture URL field with a list of URLs (`pictureUrls`). This change is not backward compatible. Therefore, we need to create a new version of our service to ensure that existing clients will continue working. To do so, we include the version in resource URIs.

With this approach, `/rooms/{roomId}` becomes `/v{versionNumber}/rooms/{roomId}`. For example, the URI for a room with ID #1 in our first API is `/v1.0/rooms/1`, and it will contain the `pictureUrl` field. The room in our new version will be accessible with `/v1.1/rooms/1` and return the list of picture URLs.

A good practice with URI-based versions is to alias non-version URIs to the latest API version. So, if the latest version of our API is 2.0, `/rooms/1` should be an alias of `/v2.0/rooms/1`.

Representation versioning

In the previous example, we produced different representations of our `Rooms`. We could therefore consider managing versioning with MIME type versioning. The following code snippet illustrates how we can achieve this with Spring Web:

```
@RequestMapping(value = "/{roomId}", method = RequestMethod.GET)
public RoomDTO getRoom(@PathVariable("roomId") long id) {
  Room room = inventoryService.getRoom(id);
  return new RoomDTO(room);
}


@RequestMapping(value = "/{roomId}", method = RequestMethod.GET,
  consumes = "application/json;version=2")
public RoomDTOv2 getRoomV2(@PathVariable("roomId") long id) {
  Room room = inventoryService.getRoom(id);
  return new RoomDTOv2(room);
}
```

With this setup, `getRoomV2()` will be invoked when requests have their Content-Type headers set to `application/json;version=2`. Otherwise, `getRoom()` will handle requests for the access of rooms.

Other approaches

Besides the two approaches described previously, one could consider using other solutions. For example, a dedicated header, such as X-API-Version, could be used to specify which API version should be used. The following code will handle requests to get rooms for version 3 of our API:

```
@RequestMapping(value = "/{roomId}", method = RequestMethod.GET,
  headers = {"X-API-Version=3"})
public RoomDTOv3 getRoomV3(@PathVariable("roomId") long id) {
  Room room = inventoryService.getRoom(id);
  return new RoomDTOv3(room);
}
```

In this example, we instructed Spring to map requests to /rooms/{roomId} containing the header, X-API-Version, with a value of 3 for this method.

Whichever technique one chooses to employ, API designers should bear the following principles in mind:

- Expose only what is required; maintaining backward compatibility is hard work.

- Favor forward-compatible changes over breaking ones. It is not always possible to force clients to upgrade to new API versions.

- From the onset, design APIs with support for evolutions. Depending on the selected approach, back-porting such support into an API might not be straightforward.

Summary

Over the course of this chapter, we found out about the Data-Transfer-Object design pattern. We looked at good practices for designing responses, and how to control their format. Finally, we discussed versioning and how it can be used in practice to manage API evolutions.

It is now time to move on with the implementation of our sample property management system web service. In the next chapter, we will delve into how CRUD operations can be handled in a RESTful web service with Spring Web.

5
CRUD Operations in REST

In *Chapter 3*, *The First Endpoint*, we created our first RESTful endpoint to access rooms in our sample property management system. Requests to retrieve data are typically mapped to the HTTP GET method in RESTful web services.

Now, we will expand on this previous example and implement the remaining endpoints to support all CRUD (Create, Read, Update, and Delete) operations.

In this chapter, we will cover the following topics:

- Mapping CRUD operations to HTTP methods
- Creating resources
- Updating resources
- Deleting resources
- Testing RESTful operations
- Emulating PUT and DELETE methods

Mapping CRUD operations to HTTP methods

The HTTP 1.1 specification defines the following methods:

- OPTIONS: This method represents a request for information about the communication options available to the requested **URI**. This is, typically, not directly leveraged with REST. However, this method can be used as part of the underlying communication. For example, this method may be used when consuming web services from a web page (as part of the cross-origin resource sharing mechanism).

- GET: This method retrieves the information identified by the requested URI. In the context of RESTful web services, this method is used to retrieve resources. As illustrated in *Chapter 3*, *The First Endpoint*, this is the method used for read operations (the R in CRUD).

- HEAD: These requests are semantically identical to GET requests except that the body of the response is not transmitted. This method is useful for obtaining meta-information about resources. Similar to the OPTIONS method, this method is usually not used directly in REST web services.

- POST: This method is used to instruct the server to accept the entity enclosed in the request as a new resource. Create operations are typically mapped to this HTTP method.

- PUT: This method requests the server to store the enclosed entity under the request URI. To support updating REST resources, this method can be leveraged. As per the HTTP specification, the server can create the resource if the entity does not exist. It is up to the web service designer to decide whether this behavior should be implemented, or if resource creation should only be handled by POST requests.

- DELETE: The last operation not yet mapped is for the deletion of resources. The HTTP specification defines a DELETE method that is semantically aligned with the deletion of RESTful resources.

- TRACE: This method is used to perform actions on web servers. These actions are often aimed at aiding the development and testing of HTTP applications. TRACE requests aren't usually mapped to any particular RESTful operations.

- CONNECT: This HTTP method is defined to support HTTP tunneling through a proxy server. Since it deals with transport layer concerns, this method has no natural semantic mapping to RESTful operations.

The RESTful architecture does not mandate the use of HTTP as the communication protocol. Furthermore, even if HTTP is selected as the underlying transport, no provisions are made regarding the mapping of RESTful operations to HTTP methods. Developers could feasibly support all operations through POST requests.

That being said, the following CRUD to HTTP method mapping is commonly used in REST web services:

Operation	HTTP Method
Create	POST
Read	GET
Update	PUT
Delete	DELETE

Our sample web service will use these HTTP methods for supporting CRUD operations. The rest of this chapter will illustrate how to build such operations.

Creating resources

The inventory component of our sample property management system deals with rooms. In *Chapter 3*, *The First Endpoint*, we built an endpoint to access rooms. Let's take a look at how to define an endpoint for creating new resources:

```
@RestController
@RequestMapping("/rooms")
public class RoomsResource {

  @RequestMapping(method = RequestMethod.POST)
  public ApiResponse addRoom(@RequestBody RoomDTO room) {
    Room newRoom = createRoom(room);
    return new ApiResponse(Status.OK, new RoomDTO(newRoom));
  }
}
```

We've added a new method to our `RoomsResource` class to handle the creation of new rooms. As described in *Chapter 3*, *The First Endpoint*, `@RequestMapping` is used to map requests to the Java method. Here, we map `POST` requests to `addRoom()`.

 Not specifying a value (path) in `@RequestMapping` is equivalent to using "/".

We pass the new room as a `@RequestBody` annotation. This annotation instructs Spring to map the body of the incoming web request to the method parameter. Jackson is used here to convert the JSON request body to a Java object.

With this new method, POSTing requests to `http://localhost:8080/rooms` with the following JSON body will result in the creation of a new room:

```
{
  name: "Cool Room",
  description: "A room that is very cool indeed",
    room_category_id: 1
}
```

Our new method will return the newly created room:

```
{
  "status":"OK",
  "data":{
    "id":2,
    "name":"Cool Room",
    "room_category_id":1,
    "description":"A room that is very cool indeed"
  }
}
```

We could decide to only return the ID of the new resource in responses to resource creation. However, since we may sanitize or otherwise manipulate the data sent over, it is good practice to return the full resource.

Quickly testing endpoints

Chapter 8, Testing RESTful Web Services, will cover at length how to effectively test a RESTful web service, but for the purpose of quickly testing our newly created endpoint, let's take a look at testing how we can create new rooms using Postman.

Postman (`https://www.getpostman.com`) is a Google Chrome plugin extension that provides tools to build and test web APIs.

The following screenshot illustrates how Postman can be used to test this endpoint:

In Postman, we specify that we send the POST request to the URL (http://
localhost:8080/rooms) with the content type header (application/json) and
the body of the request. Sending this request illustrated as follows will result in a
new room being created and returned:

```
Body   Cookies   Headers (4)   Tests        Status 200 OK  Time  180 ms

Pretty  Raw  Preview      JSON ∨    ≡|                                    ⧉  Q

1 ▾ {
2       "status": "OK",
3 ▾     "data": {
4           "id": 4,
5           "name": "Anothor Cool Room",
6           "room_category_id": 1,
7           "description": "A room that is very cool indeed"
8       }
9   }
```

We have successfully added a room to our inventory service, using Postman. It is
equally easy to create incomplete requests to ensure that our endpoint performs any
necessary sanity checks before persisting data into the database.

Chapter 8, Testing RESTful Web Services, will discuss other approaches for testing
RESTful web services.

JSON versus form data

Posting forms is the traditional way of creating new entities on the web, and it could
easily be used to create new RESTful resources. We could change our method to the
following:

```
@RequestMapping(method = RequestMethod.POST, consumes =
   MediaType.APPLICATION_FORM_URLENCODED_VALUE)
public ApiResponse addRoom(String name, String description,
   long roomCategoryId) {
   Room room = createRoom(name, description, roomCategoryId);
   return new ApiResponse(Status.OK, new RoomDTO(room));
}
```

The main difference with the previous method is that we tell Spring to map form requests (that is, with the content type, `application/x-www-form-urlencoded`) instead of JSON requests. In addition, rather than expecting an object as a parameter, we receive each field individually.

> By default, Spring will use the Java method attribute names to map incoming form inputs. Developers can change this behavior by annotating an attribute with `@RequestParam("...")` to specify the input name.

In situations where the main web service consumer is a web application, using form requests may be more applicable. In most cases, however, the former approach is more in line with RESTful principles and should be favored. Besides, when complex resources are handled, form requests will prove cumbersome to use. From a developer's standpoint, it is easier to delegate object mapping to a third-party library such as Jackson.

Now that we have created a new resource, let's see how we can update it.

Updating resources

Choosing URI formats is an important part of designing RESTful APIs. As seen earlier, rooms are accessed using the path, `/rooms/{roomId}`, and created under `/rooms`. And you might recall that as per the HTTP specification, PUT requests can result in creating entities if they do not exist. The decision to create new resources on update requests is up to the service designer. It does, however, affect the choice of path to use for such requests.

Semantically, PUT requests update entities stored under the supplied request URI. This means that update requests should use the same URI as GET requests: `/rooms/{roomId}`. However, this approach hinders the ability to support resource creation on update, since no room identifier is available.

The alternative path we can use is `/rooms`, with the room identifier passed in the body of the request. With this approach, PUT requests can be treated as POST requests when the resource does not contain an identifier.

Given that the first approach is semantically more accurate, we will choose not to support resource creation on update, and we will use the following path for PUT requests: `/rooms/{roomId}`.

The update endpoint

The following method provides the necessary endpoint to modify rooms:

```
@RequestMapping(value = "/{roomId}", method = RequestMethod.PUT)
public ApiResponse updateRoom(@PathVariable long roomId,
  @RequestBody RoomDTO updatedRoom) {
  try {
    Room room = updateRoom(updatedRoom);
    return new ApiResponse(Status.OK, new RoomDTO(room));
  } catch (RecordNotFoundException e) {
    return new ApiResponse(Status.ERROR, null, new ApiError(999,
      "No room with ID " + roomId));
  }
}
```

As discussed at the beginning of this chapter, we map update requests to the HTTP PUT verb. Annotating this method with `@RequestMapping(value = "/{roomId}", method = RequestMethod.PUT)` instructs Spring to direct PUT requests here.

The room identifier is part of the path and mapped to the first method parameter. In similar fashion to resource creation requests, we map the body to our second parameter with the use of `@RequestBody`.

Testing update requests

With Postman, we can quickly create a test case to update the room that we created earlier. To do so, we send a PUT request with the following body:

```
{
  id: 2,
  name: "Cool Room",
  description: "A room that is really very cool indeed",
    room_category_id: 1
}
```

And the resulting response will be the updated room:

```
{
  "status": "OK",
  "data": {
    "id": 2,
    "name": "Cool Room",
    "room_category_id": 1,
    "description": "A room that is really very cool indeed."
  }
}
```

Should we attempt to update a non-existent room, the server will generate the following response:

```
{
  "status": "ERROR",
  "error": {
    "error_code": 999,
    "description": "No room with ID 3"
  }
}
```

Since we do not support resource creation on update, the server returns an error indicating that the resource cannot be found.

Refer to *Chapter 4, Data Representation*, for discussions on error handling and response formats.

Deleting resources

It will come as no surprise that we use the DELETE verb to delete REST resources. Also, you will have already figured out that the path to delete requests is /rooms/ {roomId}.

The Java method that deals with room deletion is shown as follows:

```
@RequestMapping(value = "/{roomId}", method = RequestMethod.DELETE)
public ApiResponse deleteRoom(@PathVariable long roomId) {
  try {
    Room room = inventoryService.getRoom(roomId);
    inventoryService.deleteRoom(room.getId());
    return new ApiResponse(Status.OK, null);
  } catch (RecordNotFoundException e) {
    return new ApiResponse(Status.ERROR, null,
    new ApiError(999, "No room with ID " + roomId));
  }
}
```

By declaring the request mapping method to be RequestMethod.DELETE, Spring will make this method handle DELETE requests.

Since the resource is deleted, returning it in the response would not make a lot of sense. Service designers may choose to return a Boolean flag to indicate that the resource was successfully deleted. In our case, we leverage the status element of our response to carry that information back to the consumer (see *Chapter 4, Data Representation*, for more details on response formats). The response to deleting a room will be as follows:

```
{
    "status": "OK"
}
```

With this operation, we now have a full-fledged CRUD API for our Inventory Service. Before we conclude this chapter, let's discuss how REST developers can deal with situations in which not all HTTP verbs can be utilized.

Overriding the HTTP method

In certain situations (for example, when the service or its consumers are behind an overzealous corporate firewall, or if the main consumer is a web page), only the GET and POST HTTP methods might be available. In such a case, it is possible to emulate the missing verbs by passing a custom header in the requests.

For example, resource updates can be handled using POST requests by setting a custom header (for example, X-HTTP-Method-Override) to PUT to indicate we are emulating a PUT request via a POST request. The following method will handle this scenario:

```
@RequestMapping(value = "/{roomId}", method = RequestMethod.POST,
    headers = {"X-HTTP-Method-Override=PUT"})
public ApiResponse updateRoomAsPost(@PathVariable("roomId") long
    id, @RequestBody RoomDTO updatedRoom) {
    return updateRoom(id, updatedRoom);
}
```

By setting the headers attribute on the mapping annotation, Spring request routing will intercept POST requests with our custom header and invoke this method. Normal POST requests will still map to the Java method that we put together to create new rooms.

Summary

In this chapter, we continued the implementation of our sample RESTful web service by adding all the CRUD operations necessary for managing room resources. We discussed how to organize URIs to best embody the REST principles, and also looked at how to quickly test endpoints using Postman. Now that we have a fully functioning component of our system, we can take some time to discuss performance.

In the next chapter, we will look at how to manage the performance of RESTful endpoints, which techniques can be employed, and the things to watch out for.

6
Performance

In order to deploy a RESTful web service in a commercial environment, a number of criteria must be met. One of these criteria is performance. Besides yielding the correct result, RESTful endpoints must do so in a timely manner. This chapter discusses how these concerns can be addressed in real world web services. Performance optimization techniques can be applied to different aspects of a web application. However, in this chapter, we will focus on the RESTful (web) layer. *Chapter 10, Scaling a RESTful Web Service*, explores techniques that apply to other aspects of web applications. The following topics will be covered in the next few pages:

- Using HTTP compression
- Using HTTP **Cache-Control** directives
- Using HTTP **ETag** headers
- Using HTTP `Last-Modified`/`If-Modified-Since` headers

To illustrates these techniques, we will build the room availability component of our sample property management system web service

HTTP compression

While communicating with a remote service, an unavoidable amount of time is spent sending and receiving data over the network. To reduce the network latency from an application's point of view, service designers can ensure that the number of round trips is kept to a minimum. This is the subject of the remainder of this chapter. For now, however, let's take a look at another technique that can be employed to reduce the amount of data that is sent across the wire. The HTTP specification defines a mechanism for applying compression algorithms over responses before being transmitted to clients.

Content negotiation

HTTP compression revolves around content negotiation between the two parties (the server and the client). The client must notify the server about what compression algorithms it supports. Typically, these would be **deflate** and **gzip**. Clients do so by adding the following header to requests:

```
"Accept-Encoding": "gzip, deflate"
```

If the server supports one of these compression schemes, it can apply the scheme to the outgoing data. If the data is compressed, the server should add the following header to responses:

```
"Content-Encoding": "gzip"
```

With that information, the client is able to process response data appropriately.

gzip or deflate?

Other compression schemes can be used with HTTP, but gzip and deflate are the most common. So, the question is which one should service designers prefer? Unfortunately, there is some confusion about namings in the HTTP specification. Deflate and gzip actually use the same compression algorithm. gzip is a data format that leverages deflate (the algorithm) for compression. In the context of HTTP, deflate refers to Zlib, which is another data format that uses deflate. In technical terms, the deflate scheme offers better performance but is less widely supported than gzip. Therefore, gzip is the more prevalent choice for HTTP compression.

gzip compression in RESTful web services

Now that we know gzip is the more prevalent choice for HTTP compression, we want to support gzip compression in our RESTful web service. Let's take a look at how this can be achieved.

In general, it falls under the responsibility of the servlet container (for example, Tomcat, Jetty, JBoss, and so on) to deal with compression. You should refer to the documentation of these containers for details on enabling compression.

Spring Boot

If the web service uses Spring Boot and runs on either Tomcat or Jetty, enabling gzip compression is as easy as adding the following two properties in `application.properties`:

```
server.compression.enabled=true
server.compression.mime-types=application/json
```

The former property turns compression on, whereas the latter ensures that compression is applied to the JSON content.

 gzip compression works best when applied to uncompressed content. Indeed, applying gzip compression to already compressed content, such as images, is unlikely to yield any data size reduction, while wasting CPU cycles.

HTTP caching

When the topic of performance optimization is evoked, caching is often the first technique that comes to mind. Such a technique can be applied to different layers of a web service. In this section, we will focus on leveraging HTTP caching to improve performance. *Chapter 10, Scaling a RESTful Web Service*, discusses other forms of caching.

Cache-Control

Cache-Control directives are supported by HTTP to prevent unnecessary round trips between clients and servers. After all, the best way to reduce request latency is to not have to contact the server to fetch the response. These directives define who can cache responses, under which conditions, and for how long.

Private/Public caching

If, for example, a resource can safely be cached on the client for a period of time, service designers can choose to set the Cache-Control header to indicate such behavior.

Service designers must select if the caching is either private or public. They can do so by setting the appropriate value in the Cache-Control header:

```
"cache-control": "public"
```

`Public` indicates that the response may be cached by any intermediate cache. It also implies that content that is normally non-cacheable, for example, responses with HTTP authentication, may be cached.

On the other hand, `private` responses can be cached by web browsers, but they are typically only relevant to single users. In this mode, intermediates do not cache the content.

To specify how long the content should be cached, the `max-age` directive can be specified:

```
"cache-control": "private, max-age=300"
```

Responses containing this header can be cached by the user's web browser for up to 5 minutes (300 seconds).

No caching

For dynamic resources, caching might not be appropriate. In such circumstances, responses should contain the following header:

```
"cache-control": "no-cache"
```

This will instruct the browser/client to check with the server every time a request is issued. This header is often used in combination with the ETag header, as will be discussed later in this chapter.

In situations where caching must altogether be disabled, the `no-store` value should be used:

```
"cache-control": "no-store"
```

This header notifies proxies and clients not to keep a cache of responses and always go back to the server when new requests are issued.

> The Cache-Control header is part of the HTTP/1.1 specification. Older browsers and proxies might not fully support it. A common workaround is to use the **Pragma** header (part of the HTTP/1.0 spec), instead of Cache-Control.

While disabling HTTP caching is relevant in some circumstances, when, for example, sensitive data is included in the response, it should be enabled wherever applicable. Besides using the `max-age` directive, a more sophisticated solution can be created using ETag headers. The next section discusses the use of this header.

ETags

ETags provide a mechanism for validating cached responses. This makes caches more efficient and ultimately improves service response times. Upon issuing a response, the server generates a token that encapsulates the state of the resource:

```
"ETag": "xyz123"
```

When clients need to re-issue a new request for a cached response, they can include the ETag in the form of an If-None-Match header:

```
"If-None-Match": "xyz123"
```

The server can then compare this header with the current state of the resource. If the resource has changed, the server can issue a response with a new resource. Otherwise, the server can return a **304 Not Modified** response.

Last-Modified/If-Modified-Since headers

These headers offer a mechanism similar to ETags in the way that it allows clients to validate the state of cached responses. Instead of generating a hash of a resource, a time stamp is used and compared to work out whether cached responses are valid.

Now that we have introduced the technical concepts behind HTTP caching, let's put them into practice in the availability component of our sample RESTful web service.

Room availability

In previous chapters, we discussed the inventory component of our property management service. The next component we will implement is the availability service.

An overview of implementation

The aim of this component is to provide end users and third-party systems with a way to query whether rooms are available during a given period.

We will implement this functionality by looking up all the rooms in our sample property, and overlaying the existing bookings for a given period so as to work out availability. In real systems used in large hotels, more sophisticated algorithms are used to optimize room allocations. In our case, however, a simpler approach is sufficient. So, let's consider the following service interface:

```
public interface AvailabilityService {

    /**
     * Answers the availability status for the given query.
     *
     * @param query the availability query
     *
     * @return the availability status for each day in the requested
     *   period.
     */
    public List<AvailabilityStatus> getAvailableRooms(
        AvailabilityQuery query);
}
```

This service takes an availability query and returns the rooms that are available for a given period. Users will be able to query availability for the period of time and optional room category.

 The implementation of this service and associated classes can be downloaded from the Packt Publishing website.

The REST resource

Let's now consider the endpoint that we need to create to expose this functionality through a RESTful API. One fundamental question to answer, before proceeding with the implementation of this endpoint, is what URL will this resource be made available under? One possible approach would be to add a new endpoint to our existing rooms resource (see *Chapter 3, The First Endpoint*). However, since we will not be just returning a list of rooms, it isn't the most logical solution. Besides, for scalability purposes, we might want to deploy this component on a separate architecture from the Inventory Service (these concerns are discussed in *Chapter 10, Scaling a RESTful Web Service*). Therefore, we will use a new resource exposed under a new URL:

```
@RestController
@RequestMapping("/availability")
```

```
public class AvailabilityResource {

  @RequestMapping(method = RequestMethod.GET)
  public ApiResponse getAvailability(
    @RequestParam("from") String from,
    @RequestParam("until") String until,
    @RequestParam(value = "roomCategoryId", required = false) String
      categoryId) {
    // omitted
  }
}
```

With this new Spring RestController, room availability can be retrieved with URLs such as http://localhost:8080/availability?from=2016-12-01&until=2016-12-01.

This URL will return the list of available rooms on December 1, 2016.

> It is up to the developer to decide in which format to represent dates. For example, dates can be accepted in UNIX times (https://en.wikipedia.org/wiki/Unix_time). In our case, we chose to represent dates in the ISO 8601 format (https://en.wikipedia.org/wiki/ISO_8601), as it is more human-readable.

Also, we have defined a query parameter called roomCategoryId, which is optional. With Spring, we can do so with the following annotation:

```
@RequestParam(value = "roomCategoryId", required = false)
```

As we have seen in *Chapter 5, CRUD Operations in REST*, this annotation instructs Spring to map, if present, the query parameter, roomCategoryId, to our Java method parameter.

> Without declaring this request parameter as not required, Spring will generate an error response with the HTTP status 400, if the parameter is not present in the URL.

Requesting availability for a given day will return data as follows:

```
{
    "status": "OK",
    "data":   [{
      "date": "2016-12-01",
      "rooms":   [{
        "id": 1,
        "name": "Room 1",
        "roomCategoryId": 1,
        "description": "Nice, spacious double bed room with usual
          amenities"
      }]
    }]
}
```

As per our brief, this response lists the available rooms per date for the requested time period. In this case, the room with ID 1 is available on December 1, 2016.

With the RESTful endpoint defined, let's look at how we can add support for HTTP caching.

Adding HTTP caching

As discussed at the beginning of this chapter, there are several caching approaches available with HTTP. In this section, we will use the `Last-Modified`/`If-Modified-Since` headers to prevent sending unnecessary data across the wire. To do so, we need access to the HTTP response. Let's modify our endpoint:

```
@RequestMapping(method = RequestMethod.GET)
public ApiResponse getAvailability(
  @RequestParam("from") String from,
  @RequestParam("until") String until,
  @RequestParam(value = "roomCategoryId", required = false) String
    categoryId, WebRequest request) {
  // omitted
}
```

Spring will map the new attribute to the `org.springframework.web.context.request.WebRequest` object that represents the request.

The next step is to be able to work out a date that captures the current state of the response. In our case, we can use the update date of the booking that was most recently updated in the requested period.

Then, in the method body of our endpoint, we can leverage Spring's support for caching, which is shown as follows:

```
AvailabilityQuery query = new AvailabilityQuery(dateRange,
    categoryId);
// we use the last updated booking date as our Last Modified value
Date lastUpdatedBooking = getLastModified(query);
if (request.checkNotModified(lastUpdatedBooking.getTime())) {
    return null;
}
// perform the query and return the availability status
```

With the use of `WebRequest.checkNotModified()`, we compare the `If-Modified-Since` request header value with the one we computed. If the values match, we do not need to process the request, and Spring will return a 304 response. Otherwise, we can carry on and process the availability request and include our generated `Last-Modified` header.

 Invoking `checkNotModified()` will ensure that the relevant HTTP headers are set on the response. Therefore, if the data has not changed, no further processing is required and developers can safely return `null`, instead of manually constructing a 304 response.

For example, if a new user requests availability for the first time, the server will respond with the following headers:

```
HTTP/1.1 200 OK
Server: Apache-Coyote/1.1
Last-Modified: Sun, 14 Jun 2015 22:00:00 GMT
Content-Type: application/json;charset=UTF-8
Transfer-Encoding: chunked
Date: Mon, 15 Jun 2015 12:12:32 GMT
```

Upon re-issuing the same request, the user's browser will include the following headers:

```
GET /availability?from=2016-12-01&until=2016-12-01 HTTP/1.1
// omitted
If-Modified-Since: Sun, 14 Jun 2015 22:00:00 GMT
```

The server will then be able to compare the time stamp provided in the request with our last modified date and issue a 304 response:

```
HTTP/1.1 304 Not Modified
Server: Apache-Coyote/1.1
Date: Mon, 15 Jun 2015 12:16:03 GMT
```

This approach reduces both the amount of processing required on the server (assuming that generating the last modified date is not as expensive as processing the request) and the amount of data sent to the server, resulting in improved performance.

Caching with ETags

When generating a last modified date is not suitable, ETags can be used instead. Spring has transparent support for ETags in the form of a filter (`org.springframework.web.filter.ShallowEtagHeaderFilter`) that can be added to the REST servlet. This filter automatically generates an MD5 hash of the response.

The filter can be added in the web application descriptor (web.xml):

```
<filter>
  <filter-name>etagFilter</filter-name>
  <filter-class>
    org.springframework.web.filter.ShallowEtagHeaderFilter
  </filter-class>
</filter>
<filter-mapping>
  <filter-name>etagFilter</filter-name>
  <url-pattern>/*</url-pattern>
</filter-mapping>
```

Alternatively, when using Spring Boot, the filter can be added with a configuration class:

```
@Configuration
@EnableWebMvc
@ComponentScan
public class WebApplicationConfiguration extends
WebMvcAutoConfiguration {

  @Bean
  public Filter etagFilter() {
    return new ShallowEtagHeaderFilter();
  }
}
```

When a client issues a first availability request, the server returns the following headers:

```
HTTP/1.1 200 OK
Server: Apache-Coyote/1.1
ETag: "09f4ab0b7ca5d8280fbb890a6a5e1c220"
Content-Type: application/json;charset=UTF-8
Content-Length: 463
Date: Mon, 15 Jun 2015 12:40:31 GMT
```

Upon re-issuing the same request, the web browser will include the following headers:

```
GET /availability?from=2016-12-01&until=2016-12-01 HTTP/1.1
// omitted
If-None-Match: "09f4ab0b7ca5d8280fbb890a6a5e1c220"
```

The server will issue the following response:

```
HTTP/1.1 304 Not Modified
Server: Apache-Coyote/1.1
ETag: "09f4ab0b7ca5d8280fbb890a6a5e1c220"
Date: Mon, 15 Jun 2015 12:50:00 GMT
```

The actual response body is not sent and the browser is instructed to use its local cached copy instead. While this approach offers a transparent mechanism for caching data that has not changed, it does not help with improving performance on the server side.

Summary

This chapter has given us the chance to look at how one can leverage HTTP optimization methods to improve the performance of RESTful web services. In reducing round trips between clients and servers, as well as the amount of data sent across the wire, service designers can ensure request latencies are kept to a minimum. Other benefits of HTTP optimizations include lower operating expenses due to the reduction in bandwidth and lower power consumption for consumers of the service. This last point is quite important when consumers are mobile devices with a limited battery life.

Beyond HTTP-related optimizations, other techniques discussed in *Chapter 10, Scaling a RESTful Web Service*, can be employed to further manage web service performances. The next topic of importance when creating RESTful services is security. In the next chapter, we will take a look at how security can be handled with Spring.

Dealing with Security

Security crosses every boundary of IT systems; from physical access to data centers and server racks, to encrypting communications, and all the way to validating inputs of web services endpoints. In this chapter, we will focus on the security measures that directly affect web services. We will cover the following topics:

- The booking component of our sample RESTful web service being used to illustrate how security concerns can be addressed with Spring
- Authentication techniques
- Authorization techniques
- Input validation
- The use of encryption

The booking service

Before we delve into how to handle security with Spring, let's first discuss the component of our sample property management system that we will use in this chapter: the booking service.

As the name suggests, this component will provide the necessary functionality to take and manage bookings in our sample property management system. Let's consider the following Java interface:

```
public interface BookingService {
  /**
   * Looks up the booking with the given identifier.
   *
   * @param bookingId the booking identifier to look up
   * @return the booking with the given ID
   */
```

```
    public Booking getBooking(long bookingId);

    /**
     * Answers all bookings for the given date range.
     *
     * @param dateRange the date range to retrieve bookings for
     * @return the bookings in the given date range
     */
    public List<Booking> getBookings(DateRange dateRange);

    /**
     * Processes the given booking
     *
     * @param request the booking request
     * @return the result of the request
     */
    public BookingResponse book(BookingRequest request);
}
```

This abstraction allows us to make and retrieve bookings. Assuming that an implementation of this interface is available, we can now turn our attention to building the necessary RESTful endpoints to expose this functionality.

The REST resource

As we have seen in *Chapter 2, Building RESTful Web Services with Maven and Gradle,* we can expose the ability to retrieve a booking by identifier with the following code:

```
@RestController
@RequestMapping("/bookings")
public class BookingsResource {

  @Autowired
  private BookingService bookingService;

  @RequestMapping(value = "/{bookingId}",
    method = RequestMethod.GET)
  public BookingDTO getBooking(@PathVariable("bookingId") long
    bookingId) {
    return new BookingDTO(bookingService.getBooking(bookingId));
  }
}
```

In the following sections, we will learn how security can be applied to this endpoint.

Authentication

Authentication deals with ensuring that users are who they say they are. There are several approaches to authenticate users. This section will describe a few of the mechanisms provided by HTTP.

HTTP Basic authentication

This is the simplest form of authentication in the HTTP specification. It relies on a username and password combination being passed as an `Authorization` header to any HTTP request that mandates authentication.

When a client issues a request to an endpoint that requires authentication, the server will respond with a **HTTP 401 Not Authorized** response. The response will include the following header:

```
WWW-Authenticate: Basic realm="myRealm"
```

This header instructs the client that the user must be authenticated using the Basic scheme. Modern browsers will automatically prompt users for their credentials upon receiving such a response, and re-issue the request with the `Authorization` header. This header should contain the scheme followed by the username and password combination (in the format, `username:password`) encoded in `Base64`. For example, let's consider a request that contains the following header:

```
Authorization: Basic cmVzdDpyb2Nrcw==
```

Once decoded, the server will need to check for a user with the username, `rest`, and password, `rocks`.

> While this scheme is easy to put in place, no confidentiality measures are provided to protect the credentials. Indeed, the credentials are merely encoded, not encrypted, and can be quite easily accessed. Therefore, this scheme must be used with HTTPS to be considered secure.

Using Basic authentication with Spring

Let's take a look at how we can set up a Spring RESTful web service to support Basic authentication. First, we need to add a few new dependencies to our project:

```xml
<dependency>
    <groupId>org.springframework.security</groupId>
    <artifactId>spring-security-config</artifactId>
    <version>4.0.1.RELEASE</version>
```

```
    </dependency>
    <dependency>
      <groupId>org.springframework.security</groupId>
      <artifactId>spring-security-web</artifactId>
      <version>4.0.1.RELEASE</version>
    </dependency>
```

This will import Spring's web security module, as well as its configuration support. The next step is to configure security. We can do so in Java by declaring the following class:

```
@EnableWebSecurity
public class SecurityConfig extends WebSecurityConfigurerAdapter {

    @Autowired
    public void configureGlobal(AuthenticationManagerBuilder auth)
      throws Exception {
      auth.inMemoryAuthentication()
      .withUser("rest").password("rocks").roles("USER");
    }
    @Override
    protected void configure(HttpSecurity http) throws Exception {
      http.authorizeRequests()
      .anyRequest().authenticated()
      .and().httpBasic();
    }
}
```

This is a very simple configuration that is not production-ready but is simple enough to illustrate the configuring of Spring Security. We define one user with the username, rest, and password, rocks. We also instruct Spring to authenticate all requests using the HTTP Basic authentication scheme.

> In a real world system, users would not be stored in memory (as instructed in this example with auth. inMemoryAuthentication()), but in a database with passwords encrypted using, for example, **Bcrypt** encryption (https://en.wikipedia.org/wiki/Bcrypt).

The last step remaining is to get our web service to use this security configuration. We can do so by extending `org.springframework.security.web.context.AbstractSecurityWebApplicationInitializer` as follows:

```
public class SecurityWebApplicationInitializer extends
AbstractSecurityWebApplicationInitializer {

  public SecurityWebApplicationInitializer() {
    super(SecurityConfig.class);
  }
}
```

Passing our security configuration class to the super class will ensure that all requests to our sample web service will be secured.

HTTP Digest authentication

Similar to the HTTP Basic authentication scheme, the HTTP `Digest` authentication scheme uses a username and password to authenticate users. However, unlike the previous scheme, the credentials are not sent over the network in an easy-to-decode format. Instead, an **MD5** hash of the username, password, and a few extra pieces of information are sent. When the server receives the request, it generates another hash using the same algorithm and compares the two values. If they match, the user has entered the correct password. If not, the authentication has failed and the appropriate status code will be returned.

To set up `Digest` authentication in Spring, a `org.springframework.security.web.authentication.www.DigestAuthenticationFilter` filter must be configured. This filter will issue authentication headers such as:

```
WWW-Authenticate: Digest realm="My Realm", qop="auth",

nonce="MTQzNDUzMjIyNTE3MDplZjRmYzFmYzZkNDZkNDE4NzE2ZmRkNzAzMmM2YmM
0ZQ=="
```

The filter will also handle any `Authorization` headers in requests. For example:

```
Authorization: Digest username="rest", realm="My Realm",

nonce="MTQzNDUzMjM0OTk2MzoyNjQwOTA0MDI0MTEzN2E2ZjIzOGMxZDU0ZTlk
Y2MxYQ==", uri="/bookings/3",
response="1bc4974dd8ca156568149f3944cf42c8", qop=auth,
nc=00000001, cnonce="6ae950660ea900bf"
```

Upon accessing a secure resource, the service sends a WWW-Authenticate header with the scheme, realm, and extra information in a 401 response. Browsers will handle this by prompting the user and re-issuing the request with an Authorization header containing the MD5 hash of the user's credentials.

To enable Digest authentication, let's modify our SecurityConfig class:

```
@EnableWebSecurity
public class SecurityConfig extends WebSecurityConfigurerAdapter {

  @Override
  protected void configure(HttpSecurity http) throws Exception {
    http.authorizeRequests()
    .anyRequest().authenticated()
    .exceptionHandling()
    .authenticationEntryPoint(digestEntryPoint())
    .and()
    .addFilter(digestAuthenticationFilter());
  }
  // rest of the code omitted for clarity
}
```

With this updated implementation, we swap Basic authentication for the more secure Digest authentication scheme.

 While HTTP Digest authentication provides a mechanism to send encrypted credentials over an otherwise non-secure network, the reader should be aware that the MD5 algorithm has known limitations and should be considered carefully. More information can be found at https://en.wikipedia.org/wiki/Digest_access_authentication.

Token-based authentication

The last scheme we will briefly discuss is token-based authentication. This approach is not part of the HTTP specification but is a common method of authentication. This scheme relies on an encrypted token being issued by the server and subsequently sent over on every request by the client. The token can be encrypted using modern, robust encryption algorithms. Spring offers good support for such a scheme with the use of org.springframework.security.core.token.TokenService and org.springframework.security.core.token.Token.

For example, service developers can take a look at `org.springframework.security.core.token.KeyBasedPersistenceTokenService` for a sample use of this authentication approach.

Other authentication methods

If the previous authentication approaches are not a good fit, web service designers may be interested in investigating the use of the following:

- **OAuth2**: This is an open source standard of authorization that provides client applications with secure access to server resources on behalf of users. This is especially popular when users want to log in to services through third party apps. Take a look at `http://oauth.net/2/` for more details.

- **JWT**: JSON Web Token is a simple mechanism used to check whether information sent in requests can be verified and trusted using a digital signature. More information on JWT can be found at `http://jwt.io`.

Having covered authentication, we can now focus on how to manage authorization.

Authorization

The corollary to authentication is authorization. These two concepts are often handled together, but they refer to two different requirements for securing web services. Authentication validates the identity of users, whereas authorization manages which operations users are entitled to perform. Authorization often relies on associating users with roles and controlling which user roles are allowed to perform specific operations.

Authorization with Spring

There are two approaches to manage authorization with Spring:

- URL mapping
- Resource annotations

The following sections provide illustrations of these two approaches.

URL mapping

Expanding on our previous example, we can modify `SecurityConfig` to declare fine-grain URL mappings as follows:

```
@EnableWebSecurity
public class SecurityConfig extends WebSecurityConfigurerAdapter {
  @Override
  protected void configure(HttpSecurity http) throws Exception {
    http.authorizeRequests()
    .antMatchers(HttpMethod.GET, "/bookings/**").hasRole("ADMIN")
    .anyRequest().authenticated();
  }
}
```

With this new version, we instruct Spring to only allow administrators access to read bookings. All other endpoints accept requests from authenticated users with any role. To be able to test this security configuration, let's add an administrator user. We can do so by modifying our class as follows:

```
@EnableWebSecurity
public class SecurityConfig extends WebSecurityConfigurerAdapter {
  @Autowired
  public void configureGlobal(AuthenticationManagerBuilder auth)
  throws Exception {
    auth.inMemoryAuthentication()
    .withUser("rest").password("rocks").roles("USER")
    .and()
    .withUser("admin").password("admin").roles("ADMIN");
  }
}
```

Along with our rest user, we have now declared an administrator user with the username, admin, and password, admin.

With this new configuration, if we log in as a USER and try to access a booking, the server will generate a **403 Forbidden** response. Locally, you can test this with behavior by opening `http://localhost:8080/bookings/1` in a web browser.

Because the browser caches credentials with HTTP `Basic` or HTTP `Digest` authentication schemes, logging out is a bit tricky and often requires closing the browser. Thankfully, modern browsers allow private browsing. This feature can help speed up development and test the security of web services.

This approach helps secure web services globally, but might prove cumbersome when fine-grain authorization is required. Indeed, the configuration (either in Java, or XML) may become hard to maintain. A more scalable approach is described in the next section.

Resource annotations

Unlike a centralized configuration, such as the one discussed in the previous section, using annotations allows the controlling of resource access directly in the resource classes. Spring offers an expression-based access control mechanism with the use of `org.springframework.security.access.prepost.PreAuthorize`.

Let's modify the endpoint that we described at the beginning of this chapter:

```
@RestController
@RequestMapping("/bookings")
public class BookingsResource {

  @PreAuthorize("hasRole('ROLE_ADMIN')")
  @RequestMapping(value = "/{bookingId}",
    method = RequestMethod.GET)
    public BookingDTO getBooking(@PathVariable("bookingId") long
      bookingId) {
    // omitted
  }
}
```

Adding `@PreAuthorize("hasRole('ADMIN')")` to our endpoint declaration instructs Spring Security to only grant access of this resource to administrators. If a user attempts to invoke this endpoint, the server will generate a `403 Forbidden` response.

If the resource has to be accessible to multiple roles, the following expression can be used: `hasAnyRole('role1, role2')`.

Let's now turn our attention to another aspect of security that also plays an important part: input validation. The next section looks at how input validation can be implemented with Spring.

Input validation

Besides authentication and authorization, one area of importance in building secure web services is to ensure that inputs are always validated. In addition to maintaining data integrity, doing so prevents security vulnerabilities such as a SQL injection.

Java Bean annotations

To implement input validation, we can use Java Bean validation annotations that were introduced with JavaEE 6. To illustrate their use, let's implement the endpoint to take bookings in our sample web service. Our booking service accepts requests in the form of the following Java class:

```
public class BookingRequest {

    @Min(1)
    private final long roomId;

    @NotNull
    private final DateRange dateRange;

    @Size(min = 1, max = 128)
    private final String customerName;

    @NotNull
    private CreditCardDetails creditCardDetails;
}
```

You can see here the use of `@javax.validation.constraints.Min`, `@javax.validation.constraints.NotNull` and `@javax.validation.constraints.Size`. The `@Min` annotation allows the defining of the minimum valid value for `roomId`. The `@NotNull` annotation ensures that the field has a value. Finally, the `@Size` annotation helps make sure that the customer's name is not larger than the size of the database field.

Regular expressions

Another very useful validation annotation is `@javax.validation.constraints.Pattern`. This annotation allows the validation of fields, based on regular expressions. For example, let's have a look at the `CreditCardDetails` class:

```
public class CreditCardDetails {
  @NotNull
  private String cardOwner;
  @Pattern(regexp = "\\b(?:4[0-9]{12}(?:[0-9]{3})?|" +
          "5[12345][0-9]{14}|3[47][0-9]{13}|" +
          "3(?:0[012345]|[68][0-9])[0-9]{11}|" +
          "6(?:011|5[0-9]{2})[0-9]{12}|" +
          "(?:2131|1800|35[0-9]{3})[0-9]{11})\\b")
  private String cardNumber;
  @Pattern(regexp = "[0-9]{2}/[0-9]{2}")
  private String expiration;
  @Pattern(regexp = "[0-9]{3,4}")
  private String cvv;
}
```

We've declared each field in this class with validation annotations. For example, the CVV number is validated against a regular expression that checks that the value is made of three or four digits.

> In systems with large volumes of requests, using regular expressions for input validation may add unwanted latency. Therefore, service designers should consider the pros and cons when using regular expressions.

Validating bookings

Our `BookingsResource` class should validate incoming booking requests before processing them. Let's add the following endpoint:

```
@RestController
@RequestMapping("/bookings")
public class BookingsResource {
  @RequestMapping(method = RequestMethod.POST)
  public ApiResponse book(@Valid @RequestBody BookingRequest
    request) {
    BookingResponse response = bookingService.book(request);
    return new ApiResponse(Status.OK, response);
  }
}
```

This method will be invoked when a POST request is sent to `/bookings/`. By simply adding the `@Valid` annotation to the method, Spring will ensure that the incoming booking requests are run through our defined validation rules first.

For instance, using Postman, we can send a POST request like the following:

```
{
  "roomId":1,
  "dateRange": {"from":"2017-01-01","to":"2017-01-02"},
  "customerName":"Jane Doe",
  "creditCardDetails": {
    "cardNumber": "0111-1111-1111-1111",
    "cardOwner": "John Doe",
    "expiration": "01/20",
    "cvv": "020"
  }
}
```

Since the credit card number is not valid (it starts with 0), the server will respond with a **400 Bad Response** error.

Encryption

The most common form of encryption used to secure web services and the web in general is **HTTPS**. Unlike HTTP, which exchanges data between servers and clients in plain text, HTTPS encrypts the content of requests and responses so that they appear opaque to anyone listening on the network.

The literature on HTTPS is vast and readily available. In addition, support for HTTPS in software packages and hardware that is typically used in web services deployments is abundant. For these reasons, this section will not delve further into the details of using HTTPS. With the exception of building URLs for redirection, the use of a secure communication protocol has little impact on the implementation of a RESTful web service.

Storing sensitive data

In the event of a system being compromised, another point of encryption that is essential is in the persistence layer. As mentioned earlier in this chapter, it is good practice to encrypt passwords in the database, so that even if the database gets accessed by unauthorized individuals with malicious intentions, the most sensitive information remains (somewhat) safe.

Spring offers very good support for encrypting data in databases. API designers can leverage `org.springframework.security.crypto.password.PasswordEncoder`. For instance, `org.springframework.security.crypto.bcrypt.BCryptPasswordEncoder` is a good choice for hashing passwords in the database.

Summary

The breadth of security measures that service designers may need to implement is much wider than what this chapter covers. From authenticating users, to authorizing their actions, and the use of encryption to prevent eavesdropping on sensitive information, we have covered the basic principles of securing web services with Spring.

Having considered security concerns in this chapter, another critical attribute to assess the production-readiness of a RESTful web service is testing.

In the next chapter, we will investigate which tools and techniques can be leveraged to verify that our sample RESTful web service exhibits the expected behavior.

8
Testing RESTful Web Services

Testing is an inherent aspect of building commercial software solutions. Indeed, testing should be considered at every step of the development process, and a software package should only be considered ready when the complete test suite is successful.

In this chapter, we will apply the following testing strategies to our sample RESTful web service:

- Unit testing Spring controllers
- Mocking
- Testing security
- Integration strategies
- Other forms of testing to consider

Unit testing Spring controllers

Since we declared RESTful endpoints as Java methods with annotations, normal unit testing techniques can be employed. The de facto unit testing library for Java is **JUnit**. (http://www.junit.org). JUnit is a simple framework used for writing repeatable tests. The following code snippet illustrates how one can test a RESTful endpoint:

```
public class AvailabilityResourceTest {
  @Test
  public void testGetAvailability() throws Exception {
    AvailabilityService service = ...
    AvailabilityResource resource = new
      AvailabilityResource(service);
    WebRequest request = ...
    // invalid from date
```

```
      ApiResponse response = resource.getAvailability(null,
        "2017-01-02", "1", request);
      assertEquals(Status.ERROR, response.getStatus());
      assertEquals(17, response.getError().getErrorCode());
      // from is after until
      response = resource.getAvailability("2017-01-03",
        "2017-01-02", "1", request);
      assertEquals(Status.ERROR, response.getStatus());
      assertEquals(17, response.getError().getErrorCode());
    }
  }
```

Most readers will be familiar with these types of tests. Here, we verified that the availability component of our sample property management system does not accept invalid dates. What isn't covered in this code snippet is how an instance of com.packtpub.springrest.availability.AvailabilityService and org.springframework.web.context.request.WebRequest is obtained. These two interfaces are dependencies for which we don't really want to use the real implementations. We're only interested in testing the code in our resource class. The next section discusses mocking techniques for dealing with this situation.

Mocking

We have built our sample property management system by decoupling the RESTful layer from the service implementation with the use of Java interfaces. Besides helping structure the code base and preventing tight coupling, this process also benefits unit testing. Indeed, instead of using concrete service implementations when testing the web tier of our application, we can rig mocked implementations in. For instance, consider the following unit test:

```
public class RoomsResourceTest {
  @Test
  public void testGetRoom() throws Exception {
    RoomsResource resource = new RoomsResource();
    InventoryService inventoryService = ...
    ApiResponse response = resource.getRoom(1);
    assertEquals(Status.OK, response.getStatus());
    assertNotNull(response);
    RoomDTO room = (RoomDTO) response.getData();
    assertNotNull(room);
    assertEquals("Room1", room.getName());
  }
}
```

When invoking `RoomResource.getRoom()` for an existing room, we expect non-null, successful responses containing a payload that represents that room. Rather than using the real `com.packtpub.springrest.inventory.InventoryService` implementation, which has dependencies on the database, we can create a mock implementation. This mock must exhibit predefined behavior that allows us to test for different use cases handled by `com.packtpub.springrest.inventory.web.RoomsResource`. This can be achieved in two different ways, as illustrated in the next sections.

Simple mocking

In order to provide the necessary behavior, we can simply create an anonymous implementation of the Inventory Service:

```
InventoryService inventoryService = new InventoryService() {
  @Override
  public Room getRoom(long roomId) {
    if (roomId == 1) {
      Room room = new Room();
      room.setName("Room1");
      room.setDescription("Room description");
      RoomCategory category = new RoomCategory();
      category.setName("Category1");
      category.setDescription("Category description");
      room.setRoomCategory(category);
      return room;
    } else {
      throw new RecordNotFoundException("");
    }
  }
  // rest of code omitted
};
```

With this approach, we manually implement the `InventoryService` interface and insert the code that we need. Also, we return a value of `Room` for the `roomId` value, `1`, and throw a `RecordNotFoundException` otherwise.

We have omitted the stubs for all the other methods exposed in this code snippet for the purpose of readability. But this is where the challenge lies in simple mocking. Developers have to write a lot of code that provides no value to the unit test but requires maintenance whenever new functionality is to be added to the service. This is where mocking libraries come into the picture. The next section discusses the use of such a library.

Implementation stubbing with a mocking library

There are several options when it comes to mocking libraries in Java, such as jMock (http://www.jmock.org) or EasyMock (http://easymock.org). One of the most popular is **Mockito**. Mockito is a mocking framework that lets developers write clean tests and offers a simple API. Developers can add Mockito to their Maven project by adding the following dependency to the project descriptor:

```xml
<dependency>
  <groupId>org.mockito</groupId>
  <artifactId>mockito-core</artifactId>
  <version>1.9.5</version>
  <scope>test</scope>
</dependency>
```

To illustrate how to use Mockito, take a look at the following test:

```java
@Test
public void testUpdateRoom() {
    InventoryService service = mock(InventoryService.class);
    RoomCategory category = ... // skipped for clarity
    Room room = ... // skipped for clarity
    when(service.getRoom(1)).thenReturn(room);
    when(service.getRoomCategory(anyLong()))
    .thenReturn(category);
    Room updatedRoom = ... // skipped for clarity
    updatedRoom.setDescription("It's an awesome room!");
    ApiResponse response = resource.updateRoom(1,
       new RoomDTO(updatedRoom));

    assertEquals(Status.OK, response.getStatus());
    assertEquals("It's an awesome room!", ((RoomDTO)
       response.getData()).getDescription());
}
```

This test validates that it is possible to update an existing room. Instead of implementing InventoryService ourselves, we use Mockito to create a mock implementation with mock(InventoryService.class). The next step is to instruct our mock to return a room and room category when invoked. This is achieved with when(...).thenReturn(...). This pattern adds behavior to our mock. For instance, when(service.getRoom(1)).thenReturn(room) will make our mock service return a room when InventoryService.getRoom() is invoked for the room ID 1.

Mockito and Spring

Spring offers a mechanism to automatically inject beans into classes with the use of `@org.springframework.beans.factory.annotation.Autowired`. This annotation can be used as follows:

```
@RestController
@RequestMapping("/bookings")
public class BookingsResource {

    @Autowired
    private BookingService bookingService;
}
```

At startup, Spring will look up any declared bean of the type, `InventoryService`, and inject it. This mechanism reduces the amount of boilerplate code that needs to be implemented. However, it makes testing a little trickier, as with this code, we do not have direct access to the `bookingService` instance variable. Thankfully, Mockito provides several useful annotations to circumvent this limitation. We can declare our test class as follows:

```
@RunWith(MockitoJUnitRunner.class)
public class BookingsResourceTest {

    @InjectMocks
    private BookingsResource resource;

    @Mock
    private BookingService bookingService;
}
```

The first annotation (`@org.junit.runner.RunWith`) allows us to substitute the standard JUnit runner for Mockito's. With `@org.mockito.InjectMocks`, we mark fields for injection. In addition, we annotate `bookingService` with `@org.mockito.Mock`. This will automatically generate a mock that will be injected into our instance of `BookingsResource`. We can then run our test with both the resource and service classes instantiated for us.

> Read more about Mockito on their website at http://mockito.org.

Testing security

Spring has good support for unit testing. Developers can add new dependencies to their Maven project to include Spring testing support as follows:

```
<dependency>
    <groupId>org.springframework</groupId>
    <artifactId>spring-test</artifactId>
    <version>4.1.6.RELEASE</version>
    <scope>test</scope>
</dependency>
<dependency>
    <groupId>org.springframework.security</groupId>
    <artifactId>spring-security-test</artifactId>
    <version>4.0.1.RELEASE</version>
    <scope>test</scope>
</dependency>
```

Because we don't want these dependencies to be included in the released product, we specify test as the scope. Doing so will only make the libraries available on the classpath during testing.

In *Chapter 7, Dealing with Security*, we added security to the booking component of our sample property management system. For reference, we limited the access to the RESTful endpoint to retrieve bookings as follows:

```
@PreAuthorize("hasRole('ADMIN')")
@RequestMapping(value = "/{bookingId}", method =
  RequestMethod.GET)
public ApiResponse getBooking(@PathVariable("bookingId") long
bookingId) {
    // omitted
}
```

With standard unit tests, we cannot validate that only administrators can access this endpoint. Using Spring's testing support, we can write unit tests for this endpoint as follows:

```
@RunWith(SpringJUnit4ClassRunner.class)
@ContextConfiguration("classpath:booking-test.xml")
public class BookingsResourceTest {

  @Autowired
  private BookingService bookingService;
  @Autowired
  private BookingsResource resource;
```

```
@Test (expected =
   AuthenticationCredentialsNotFoundException.class)
public void testGetBookingNotLoggedIn() throws Exception {
   resource.getBooking(1);
}

@Test (expected = AccessDeniedException.class)
@WithMockUser
public void testGetBookingNotAdmin() throws Exception {
   resource.getBooking(1);
}

@Test
@WithMockUser(roles = {"ADMIN"})
public void testGetBookingValidUser() throws Exception {
   when(bookingService.getBooking(1)).thenReturn(new Booking());
   assertNotNull(resource.getBooking(1));
}
}
```

By annotating the test class with `@org.junit.runner.RunWith`, we substitute the standard JUnit runner with Spring's.

Because no authentication is defined in `testGetBookingNotLoggedIn()`, we expect an exception to be thrown.

Our second test method declares a user, thanks to `@org.springframework.security.test.context.support.WithMockUser`. However, since the user has the role, USER, by default, we also expect an exception to be thrown.

Finally, the third test method (`testGetBookingValidUser()`) declares a user with the correct role, and therefore can proceed with retrieving the booking with ID 1.

Integration testing

Where unit testing helps with ensuring correct behavior is exhibited by the individual classes; integration testing focuses on the interaction between the different components of a system. The larger the system is, the more importance this form of testing takes on. The following two sections offer techniques to create effective integration strategies.

Continuous delivery

Continuous delivery is a software engineering practice that advocates the production of software in short cycles that can be reliably released. Traditionally, once changes are committed to the code base, a server builds the software and runs the full test suite. If successful, the software can be deployed automatically to a staging environment. Integration tests can then be executed against the new version of the software.

With Maven, we can define a simple means to separate unit tests from integration tests by their naming conventions; integration tests should have the suffix, `IntegrationTest`. The following can then be added to the project descriptor:

```
<plugin>
  <groupId>org.apache.maven.plugins</groupId>
  <artifactId>maven-surefire-plugin</artifactId>
  <configuration>
    <excludes>
      <exclude>**/*IntegrationTest.java</exclude>
    </excludes>
  </configuration>
  <executions>
    <execution>
      <id>integration-test</id>
      <goals>
        <goal>test</goal>
      </goals>
      <phase>integration-test</phase>
      <configuration>
        <excludes>
          <exclude>none</exclude>
        </excludes>
        <includes>
          <include>**/*IntegrationTest.java</include>
        </includes>
      </configuration>
    </execution>
  </executions>
</plugin>
```

With this configuration, unit tests can be run first. Integration tests can be run once the software has been deployed to a staging environment.

 Deployments occur very frequently throughout the lifetime of a software project. It is, therefore, a very good investment to spend time automating the deployment process. It will save the developer's time and facilitate continuous delivery.

Integration tests with Spring Boot

Spring Boot offers good support for integration testing using handy annotations, as illustrated in the following code snippet:

```
@RunWith(SpringJUnit4ClassRunner.class)
@SpringApplicationConfiguration(classes = WebApplication.class)
@WebAppConfiguration
@IntegrationTest("integration_server:9000")
public class BookingsResourceIntegrationTest {

  @Test
  public void runTests() {
    // ...
  }
}
```

As described previously in this chapter, the @org.junit.runner.RunWith annotation allows the use of an alternative test runner. In this case, we substitute JUnit's default runner for Spring's. In addition, we specify what address to connect to via @org.springframework.boot.test.IntegrationTest. With these annotations, we can connect to a server that is running our sample booking service and run a suite of integration tests against it.

 You should refer to the next chapter for code samples to invoke RESTful web services remotely. The same techniques can be used to implement integration tests.

Postman

As we have briefly discussed in *Chapter 5, CRUD Operations in REST*, we can leverage Postman (`https://www.getpostman.com`) to write test suites in order to validate our RESTful web service. This type of testing is, effectively, integration testing. For example, if we write a test that checks room availability through our REST API, we will be testing the availability, inventory, and booking components of our system. Postman offers the ability to define collections of tests, as illustrated by the following screenshot:

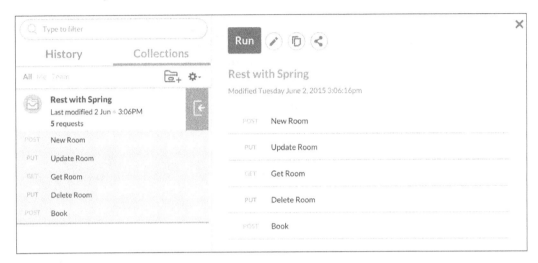

We can quickly run the entire collection of calls to a staging environment and ensure that the expected responses are returned.

 In its free version, Postman does not offer complete support for testing. Developers must obtain a license to add assertions to their calls.

Postman and security

For secure calls, such as the ones described in *Chapter 7, Dealing with Security*, we need to instruct Postman to send the correct headers. For HTTP Basic authentication, we first need to generate a Base64-encoded username and password pair (for example, `cmVzdDpyb2Nrcw==` for `rest:rocks`), and add the `Authorization` header to secure calls:

With this header added, the call will be authenticated on the server and able to proceed.

Other forms of testing

Besides unit and integration testing, other forms of testing should be considered. They are described in the next sections.

User Acceptance Testing

User Acceptance Testing (UAT) looks at testing from a user's point of view. In the case of an API, the user is a piece of software consuming the service. Regardless of the type of user, this form of testing is important to ensure that a RESTful web service exposes a consistent and feature-complete API. UAT tends to be less automated than other types of testing. However, UAT test managers should ultimately have the final say in whether a software solution is ready for general availability.

Load testing

Another important criterion in measuring the production readiness of a RESTful web service is whether it will perform in line with the expected **Service Level Agreements (SLAs)** under load. For example, during peak times, the service might be expected to handle 1,000 requests per second, with an average response time of no more than 250 milliseconds.

There are a number of commercial and open source products to test whether a web service can handle such load. The most common is the open source software, Apache JMeter (`http://jmeter.apache.org`). With JMeter, developers can create test plans that can be executed at defined rates and capture response times. The screenshot that follows shows the result of running a test plan that contains one call to our sample property management system to retrieve the room with ID, 1:

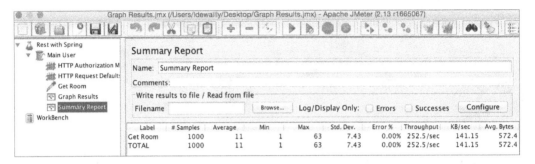

We executed `http://localhost:8080/rooms/1` 1,000 times concurrently (with 10 threads), and the average response time was 11 ms. By increasing the number of threads, we can simulate more load on the service.

Simulating real production load is not easy to achieve. Therefore, service designers may see discrepancies between performance under simulated load and real load. This fact does not take away the value of load testing. It merely suggests that service designers should not rely solely on load testing results to ensure that SLAs are met.

Summary

In this chapter, we discussed how developers can go about thoroughly testing RESTful web services. Beyond traditional unit testing, we covered security testing, integration testing, and briefly touched upon other types of testing such as UAT and load testing.

So far in this book, we have looked at web services from the server's side. However, for any such service, and indeed any piece of software, to be useful, it needs to be used. In our context, a RESTful web service is useful only if it is consumed by clients.

In the next chapter, we will look at how to build a client using Spring.

9
Building a REST Client

Having focused on the server side of RESTful web services so far, let's turn the tables and look at how we can build a client for our sample property management system with Spring. In this chapter, we will discuss the following topics:

- The basic setup for building a RESTful service client with Spring
- Invoking service endpoints
- Remote versus local clients
- Handling security
- Exception handling

Spring offers useful tools to quickly and efficiently build clients, as we will see throughout this chapter.

The basic setup

Client libraries should be self-contained and portable, so that consumers of RESTful web services may use them. It would be tempting to share code between the server side and client side. Doing so would, however, make the client and server code tightly coupled and hinder the portability of the client library.

In the context of our sample property management service, we will build the client library as a new Maven module. This module will need the following dependencies:

```
<dependency>
  <groupId>org.springframework</groupId>
  <artifactId>spring-web</artifactId>
  <version>4.1.6.RELEASE</version>
</dependency>
<dependency>
  <groupId>commons-logging</groupId>
```

```
    <artifactId>commons-logging</artifactId>
    <version>1.1.3</version>
  </dependency>
  <dependency>
    <groupId>com.fasterxml.jackson.core</groupId>
    <artifactId>jackson-databind</artifactId>
    <version>2.3.2</version>
  </dependency>
```

To build a RESTful client with Spring, we need, at minimum, a dependency on Spring's web module. In addition, Spring requires the Apache `commons-logging` library at runtime. And finally, we will leverage Jackson to perform the data binding between our Java classes and their JSON representations.

Declaring a client

With these dependencies in place, let's jump right into building a client for our sample property management system. We will start with the `Inventory` component, using the following (simplified) client interface:

```
public interface InventoryServiceClient {
  public Room getRoom(long roomId);
}
```

This interface allows the retrieving of a room by its identifier.

 The next section discusses why it is a good idea to declare our client as an interface.

We can now start implementing our client:

```
public class RemoteInventoryServiceClient implements
InventoryServiceClient {

  private final String serviceUrl;
  private final RestTemplate template;

  public RemoteInventoryServiceClient(String serviceUrl) {
    this.serviceUrl = serviceUrl;
    template = new RestTemplate();
  }

  @Override
  public Room getRoom(long roomId) {
    ParameterizedTypeReference<ApiResponse<Room>> typeReference =
      new ParameterizedTypeReference<ApiResponse<Room>>() {};
```

```
    return (Room) ResponseHandler.handle(
      () -> template.exchange(serviceUrl + "/rooms/" + roomId,
      HttpMethod.GET, null, typeReference).getBody());
  }
}
```

The main class Spring provides us with is `org.springframework.web.client.RestTemplate`. This class lets us make HTTP calls to our backend server by using `RestTemplate.exchange()`.

As discussed in *Chapter 4*, *Data Representation*, our service responses are wrapped in a common envelope format that includes information about the status of the request. Since all responses will possess the same format, we can create a utility method to handle them in a consistent manner. This is the purpose of `ResponseHandler.handle()`.

Since we use generic types to specify the type of payload responses to be contained, we need to pass that information to Spring so that it can extract the data correctly. This is achieved by declaring a `ParameterizedTypeReference`.

> Note that no particular setup is required for JSON marshaling. It will happen automatically thanks to having Jackson on the classpath.

Remote versus local clients

As we have previously seen in this chapter, our clients were defined by using interfaces. The main motivation for this added level of abstraction is so that we can substitute a remote implementation for a local one. Let's say that component A depends on component B. If these components were deployed on separate servers, we would want to use an implementation of B's client that makes remote calls to the component. If, however, both components co-existed within the same JVM, using a remote client would incur unnecessary network latency. Substituting the client for one that directly invokes component B's Java implementation ensures that no networking takes place, thus reducing latency.

> This pattern is commonly used in Microservice architectures (https://en.wikipedia.org/wiki/Microservices), which are becoming very popular. This style of architecture advocates the breaking up of complex applications into small, independent components.

Availability and booking services

Let's look at the availability and booking components of our sample property
management system. The availability service is dependent on the booking service.
To deal with this, we define a simple client interface for the booking service,
as shown here:

```
public interface BookingServiceClient {

    /**
     * Looks up the booking with the given identifier.
     *
     * @param bookingId the booking identifier to look up
     *
     * @return the booking with the given ID
     */
    public Booking getBooking(long bookingId);
}
```

This client interface defines a single method to look up a booking by its identifier.

Our first deployment approach is to have both components running in separate
JVMs. Therefore, we implement a remote client that the availability service can
leverage:

```
public class RemoteBookingServiceClient implements
  BookingServiceClient {

    private final String serviceUrl;
    private final RestTemplate template;

    public RemoteBookingServiceClient(String serviceUrl) {
        if (serviceUrl == null) {
            throw new IllegalArgumentException("serviceUrl cannot
                be null");
        }
        this.serviceUrl = serviceUrl;
        template = new RestTemplate();
    }

    @Override
    public Booking getBooking(long bookingId) {
        //omitted to clarity
        return (Booking) ResponseHandler.handle(
```

```
     () -> template.exchange(serviceUrl + "/bookings/" +
     bookingId, HttpMethod.GET, null, typeReference).getBody());
  }
}
```

In previous sections of this chapter, we've covered how to use `org.springframework.web.client.RestTemplate` to remotely invoke the service.

Now, to reduce latency, we decide to run both components in the same JVM. Using this client implementation will negate any benefit of hosting both services in the same process. Therefore, we need a new implementation:

```
public class LocalBookingServiceClient implements BookingServiceClient
{

  @Autowired
  private BookingService bookingService;

  @Override
  public Booking getBooking(long bookingId) {
    com.packtpub.springrest.model.Booking booking =
      bookingService.getBooking(bookingId);
    Booking clientBooking = new Booking();
    clientBooking.setId(booking.getId());
    // omitted setting other fields for clarity
    return clientBooking;
  }
}
```

With this new implementation, we simply delegate the booking retrieval to the actual service, bypassing any networking. We then need to transform the data into what the client invoker is expecting.

Handling security

In *Chapter 7*, *Dealing with Security*, we learned to apply security to RESTful endpoints. For instance, we discussed how to set up the HTTP `Basic` authentication for the booking service. We can expand on the previous section's example and add security handling. The next two sections illustrate how to handle both the `Basic` and `Digest` authentications.

The Basic authentication

This authentication scheme requires the `Authorization` header to contain the username/password pair encoded in Base64. This is easily achieved by modifying the client as follows:

```
public RemoteBookingServiceClient(String serviceUrl,
  String username, String password) {

  template = new RestTemplate();
  String credentials = Base64.getEncoder().encodeToString((username +
    ":" + password).getBytes());
  template.getInterceptors().add((request, body, execution) -> {
    request.getHeaders().add("Authorization", "Basic " +
    credentials);
    return execution.execute(request, body);
  });
}
```

This new constructor takes the username and password to authenticate the client. It then generates the Base64-encoded credentials and, in order to add the `Authorization` token to every request, defines a new `org.springframework.http.client.ClientHttpRequestInterceptor`. The interceptor adds the header in the appropriate format and allows the request to be executed.

The Digest authentication

For this authentication scheme, let's look at how developers can choose Apache's `HttpClient` (https://hc.apache.org) as the underlying HTTP client framework. For this purpose, we need to add the following dependency to our project:

```
<dependency>
    <groupId>org.apache.httpcomponents</groupId>
    <artifactId>httpclient</artifactId>
    <version>4.3.4</version>
</dependency>
```

And, we change the way we create our `RestTemplate` instance:

```
CredentialsProvider provider = new BasicCredentialsProvider();
CloseableHttpClient client = HttpClientBuilder.create().
  setDefaultCredentialsProvider(provider).build();
UsernamePasswordCredentials credentials = new
  UsernamePasswordCredentials(username, password);
```

```
provider.setCredentials(AuthScope.ANY, credentials);
RestTemplate template = new RestTemplate(new DigestAuthHttpRequestFact
ory(host, client));
```

By passing a request factory to our template, we are able to leverage `HttpClient` to manage the `Digest` authentication. We need to create an extension of `HttpComponentsClientHttpRequestFactory` as follows:

```
public class DigestAuthHttpRequestFactory extends
HttpComponentsClientHttpRequestFactory {

  @Override
  protected HttpContext createHttpContext(HttpMethod httpMethod,
    URI uri) {
      AuthCache authCache = new BasicAuthCache();
      authCache.put(host, new DigestScheme());
      BasicHttpContext localcontext = new BasicHttpContext();
      localcontext.setAttribute(AUTH_CACHE, authCache);
      return localcontext;
  }
}
```

This class creates an HTTP context that is set up to store the `Digest` credentials. We instruct `HttpClient` to handle authentication with the `Digest` scheme by creating a new instance of `org.apache.http.impl.auth.DigestScheme`. With this setup, our client class transparently deals with authentication in the same way that it did with the `Basic` authentication scheme in the previous section.

HTTP public key pinning

HTTP public key pinning (HPKP) is a **Trust on First Use** security technique that prevents impersonations of fraudulent SSL certificates. Responses from RESTful web services supporting HPKP will include the header, `Public-Key-Pins`, containing a hash of their SSL certificate's **Subject Public Key Information (SPKI)**. Client applications should cache this value when they first receive it, and validate any subsequent responses with the previously cached header value. If the values do not match, client applications can prevent further communication with the fraudulent server.

While the Spring Framework does not provide support for HPKP out of the box, it would be quite straightforward to implement this security feature by using a request filter.

[You can read more about HTTP public key signing at
https://en.wikipedia.org/wiki/HTTP_Public_Key_Pinning.]

Exception handling

Chapter 3, The First Endpoint, touched upon defining a consistent response format including error codes and error descriptions. The corollary on the client side is to define an exception that encapsulates information about why a particular call failed. We could, therefore, define the following exception:

```java
public class ClientException extends RuntimeException {

    private final int errorCode;
    private final String errorDescription;

    public ClientException(ApiError error) {
        super(error.getErrorCode() + ": " + error.getDescription());
        this.errorCode = error.getErrorCode();
        this.errorDescription = error.getDescription();
    }

    public int getErrorCode() {
        return errorCode;
    }

    public String getErrorDescription() {
        return errorDescription;
    }
}
```

Clients consuming a RESTful web service with such exception handling will have a consistent way to manage and report errors. There are, however, a few situations where generic exception handling requires more work on the client side. For example, the server might generate a specific error when it's unable to handle the current load and requires clients to re-issue their requests after a delay of a few seconds.

In such a situation, it would make the service consumer's job easier if they were able to catch a specific exception, rather than have to introspect the generic exception. The client implementation could declare an extension of ClientException called, for example, ServerOverloadedClientException, and throw this exception instead of the generic one where relevant.

The attentive reader will have noticed that we declared `ClientException` as an unchecked exception. This gives us the ability to manage our exception handling without exposing it.

> The decision of using checked or unchecked exceptions is often more of a personal preference than a technically motivated choice. Being required to catch an exception on every method of a client library might prove rather cumbersome. Equally, not having to catch exceptions might lead consumers to not handle error situations that they could, otherwise, recover from.

Summary

With this penultimate chapter, you have learned to build a RESTful web service client, work with authentication, as well as deal with exception handling. This nicely completes the story of building RESTful web services using the Spring Framework.

In the last and final chapter of this book, we will look at how such services can be deployed and scaled to handle large volumes of requests.

10
Scaling a RESTful Web Service

In today's world, the Internet has taken a central role. And with popular web services, such as Facebook or Twitter, handling billions of requests daily, scalability is a major challenge that service designers are facing. This chapter aims at providing ideas and techniques that can be applied by service designers to deal with scalability concerns.

In this chapter, we will discuss the following topics:

- The benefits of clustering
- Load balancing
- Distributed caching
- Asynchronous communications

Clustering

Before we look at clustering techniques, let's discuss the concepts and differences between scaling up and scaling out.

Scaling up versus scaling out

One way to deal with increased traffic is to scale a web service's underlying infrastructure vertically, or up. By leveraging the latest server architectures with powerful CPUs and sufficient memory, service designers can improve the throughput of their systems. However, this approach is bounded by the servers' physical limitations. Once these limitations are reached, throughput can no longer be improved. In addition, this approach may not make economic sense. Indeed, the cost of the latest generation of servers might prove to be prohibitive.

This technique is often used in data-tiers. Due to the deployment complexity of database sharding, it often makes more sense to scale up the persistence infrastructure. This allows you to delay the addition of this extra complexity until it is no longer avoidable.

By contrast, scaling horizontally, or out, a system revolves around leveraging commodity servers in large numbers. Instead of having one server handling all the traffic, a clustered infrastructure will rely on multiple servers, each handling only a fraction of the incoming traffic. This is what we refer to as clustering.

This approach is only possible with the use of a load balancing solution, which will be discussed later in this chapter.

The benefits of clustered systems

The obvious and main advantage of a clustered system is its ability to scale as traffic increases. That said, other benefits include the following:

- **Fault tolerance**: Because a clustered architecture relies on multiple servers, hardware failure does not (necessarily) result in a loss of service. A cluster should be provisioned to cater for the loss of at least one node.

- **High Availability**: Since multiple servers form a cluster, it is possible to perform maintenance operations, such as restarts or deployments, without downtime. Rolling restarts, for example, rely on restarting each node one at a time, moving on to the next one only when the node is back online. This means that no loss of service needs to be incurred during normal operation.

On the other hand, one of the challenges that service designers face with clustering is state management. If a system is stateless, then clustering is straightforward. If the system is stateful, however, some form of state sharing must be devised, and the complexity of clustering significantly increases. It is therefore no surprise that one of REST's principles is statelessness.

Load balancing

The most useful tool at the disposition of service designers to support clustering is a load balancer. Using a variety of algorithms (for example, round robin or least connection), a load balancer component distributes incoming requests to multiple backend servers for processing. The following diagram illustrates such an infrastructure:

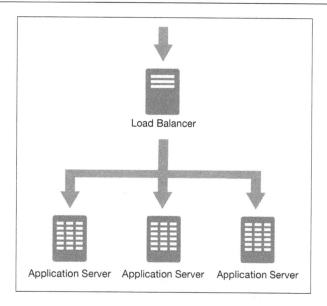

Load balancing solutions range from enterprise-grade commercial appliances, such as F5's BIG-IP (https://f5.com/products/big-ip), to open source software packages such as **HAProxy** (http://www.haproxy.org). At its core, load balancing plays a straightforward (albeit critical) role of distributing load across a fleet of backend servers. It usually does so with a form of health monitoring, so as to only forward traffic to healthy backend servers. This dynamicity has the added benefit of allowing quick scaling, up or down, of the backend infrastructure based on the volume of requests.

Besides distributing the incoming traffic, load balancers provide a level of insulation between the frontend and backend infrastructures. The frontend servers only need to know about the load balancer to pass the traffic through.

 Load-balancing solutions typically offer a form of clustering for High Availability purposes. The load-balancing infrastructure is the entry point of the entire system and must not become a single point of failure.

Linear scalability

Linear scalability refers to the idea that adding nodes to a cluster will increase the capacity at a constant rate. In other words, linear scalability implies that cluster management overheads are negligible. It is an ideal situation, but it is difficult to achieve in real world deployments. Indeed, maintaining a cluster of servers may require some form of coordination between the servers. The more the servers added to the cluster, the more the management required. In large deployments, this coordination could lead to network saturation.

Another side effect of scaling the application-tier is that the performance bottlenecks can move down to the data-tier. For example, let's consider that one external request to the service results in two database queries: one query to validate security credentials and one to retrieve the requested data. Now, let's assume an application server can handle 100 requests per second. At full capacity, the data-tier will need to handle 200 queries per second. Clustering the application-tier will result in higher throughput for that tier. If the cluster is composed of five nodes, the database will need to handle 1,000 queries per second for the overall system to scale linearly. Scaling databases is, however, not a simple exercise.

Fortunately, caching techniques can be applied to the data-tier (as well as to the application-tier) to help reduce load on the persistence layer. These techniques are discussed in the next section.

Distributed caching

Beyond the caching techniques that we discussed in *Chapter 6, Performance*, which help improve the overall latency of a RESTful web service, other caching approaches can be employed to improve the scalability of such a service.

Data-tier caching

Service designers can choose to add a caching layer on top of the database. This is a common strategy for improving (read) throughput. In our sample property management system, we use **Hibernate** to access the database. Hibernate offers two different levels of caching. They are discussed next.

First-level caching

This level is built into Hibernate as a means of reducing SQL update statements being issued. This is an in-memory cache that requires no specific setup.

Second-level caching

The second level of caching is optional and fully configurable. The caching strategy to employ can be defined per entity and multiple providers are supported out of the box:

- **Ehcache** (http://ehcache.org): This is a Java open source cache that supports caching data in memory and on disk. Ehcache can be set up as a distributed cache. It is a popular choice for second-level caching with Hibernate.

- **OSCache** (https://java.net/projects/oscache): This is a lesser-known Java caching framework. This framework is no longer under development and is listed here for the sake of completion.

- **JBoss Cache** (http://jbosscache.jboss.org): The aim of this caching framework is to provide enterprise-grade clustering solutions. It is based on the JGroups multicast library. It is fully transactional and clustered.

Application-tier caching

In addition to the data-tier caching discussed previously, API designers may also choose to apply some caching in the application-tier. For instance, the result of time-consuming computations could be stored in a cache, rather than performed on every request. For this purpose, a number of popular options exist:

- **Memcached** (http://memcached.org): This is the most common choice when it comes to distributed caching. Memcached is a free, open source, high performance object caching solution that is used in many large-scale systems. It offers a simple, generic API as well as bindings in most popular languages.

- **Redis** (http://redis.io): This is a new, more modern alternative to Memcached. It is an advanced key-value cache. Besides its caching capabilities, Redis also offers computational features. It is often preferred to Memcached for its speed and advanced capabilities.

- **Hazelcast** (http://hazelcast.org): This an open source in-memory data grid. It simplifies distributed computing by providing a simple API and a straightforward deployment strategy. Hazelcast also offers a Memcached client library, so applications using a Memcached cluster can easily write to a Hazelcast cluster.

- **Ehcache**: As described in the previous section, Ehcache provides clustered caching capabilities. It is a popular solution for small to medium scale deployments.

- **Riak** (http://basho.com/products/#riak): This is a distributed NoSQL key-value data store that offers High Availability and Fault Tolerance. Data can be stored in memory, disk, or a combination of both. Riak is written in Erlang. It trades off performance for strong data integrity guarantees.

- **Aerospike** (http://www.aerospike.com): This is an open source, real-time NoSQL database and key-value store. This flash-optimized in-memory caching solution that is written in C, offers a good compromise between performance and cost.

Which solution you should choose depends on many factors such as performance requirements, data integrity, fault tolerance, and cost. Regardless of the solution, however, adding an effective distributed caching layer to the application-tier of a web service will give designers the necessary tools to cluster their services.

Asynchronous communication

Another method to help with scalability is using an asynchronous form of communication between the components of a system. Asynchronous communication is a form of communication where a measurable amount of time passes between a request being issued and the availability of the response. For instance, a photographer's portfolio system typically requires generating thumbnails of photos, as well as watermarking originals. These processes can be time consuming, and therefore a synchronous style of communication isn't suitable. The image-processing component of this system would benefit from providing a callback mechanism that notifies you of the tasks' completion.

In addition, by adding this level of abstraction between components, we enable service designers to deal with scalability concerns independently. In the preceding example, we might require computation-optimized servers to handle image-processing tasks, while other components might only require general-purpose commodity servers.

Some possible asynchronous communication approaches include:

- **Database polling**: This technique uses a database table as a queue. The consumers poll the database at regular intervals to retrieve messages from the table.

- **Message Oriented Middleware (MOM)**: This is an infrastructure, supporting the sending and receiving of messages between distributed systems, as illustrated by the following diagram:

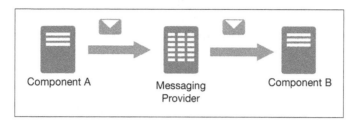

  RabbitMQ (https://www.rabbitmq.com) and **Apache ActiveMQ** (http://activemq.apache.org) are good examples of MOMs.

- **Asynchronous RESTful API**: By annotating an endpoint with @org.springframework.scheduling.annotation.Async and returning a java.util.concurrent.Future package, it is possible to build an asynchronous RESTful operation.

Now, let's look into each of the techniques in detail.

Database polling is mentioned here because this technique is used in real-world (small-scale) systems. While this technique works for low volume, small-scale systems, it is a very limited messaging approach and will perform poorly under heavy load (for example, with many consumers). It also lacks the sophistication of MOM solutions.

MOM's purpose is to provide a dedicated infrastructure for the exchange of messages between the components of a system. Such a system typically offers different communication patterns, such as producer/consumer, where consumers compete with each other for messages, and publisher/subscriber, where all the subscribers receive their own copies of messages. A MOM solution will also typically provide durability guarantees (messages are not lost in the event of a crash) and offer some administration tools.

While an asynchronous RESTful API provides some asynchronicity, it lacks many advantages that MOM-based solutions offer. Furthermore, making asynchronous calls over what is essentially a synchronous protocol (HTTP) is somewhat clunky and should only be considered if using a MOM is not an option.

In addition to helping with scalability, asynchronous communication is a great mechanism for ensuring loose coupling between components. In the case of a messaging middleware solution, each component only needs to know about where to publish messages to or where to consume them from. They do not require prior knowledge of another component's topology. Furthermore, if one component is down, messages can sit in a queue until the consuming component is available again.

Summary

Hopefully, this chapter has given the reader food for thought and techniques to apply to scale a RESTful web service. Ultimately, scaling a system is a complex exercise and no one solution fits all needs. The most important aspects for designers to bear in mind are that they should avoid single points of failure and prefer stateless systems over stateful ones to the extent that it is possible to do so (not all applications lend themselves to statelessness). Avoiding tight coupling between the components of a system through well-defined interfaces and asynchronous communication should also be high on the agenda.

This chapter also concludes our tour of building performant, secure, and scalable RESTful web services with the Spring Framework. You should now be armed with sufficient knowledge to build such a service in a commercial environment. This book will make you realize that REST is a software architecture approach that has become very popular because of its portability, simplicity, and non-reliance on heavy and complex frameworks, which is more common with SOAP-based web services.

Index

second-level caching
  about 99
  Ehcache 99
  JBoss Cache 99
  OSCache 99
security
  handling 89
  testing 78, 79
security, handling
  Basic authentication 90
  Digest authentication 90, 91
  HTTP public key pinning (HPKP) 91
Service Level Agreements (SLAs) 84
Service Module
  anatomy 12, 13
  local, versus remote service
    invocations 14
Simple Object Access Protocol (SOAP) 1
Spring
  used, for authorization 65
  using, with Mockito 77
Spring Boot
  URL 16
  using, with integration testing 81
Spring controllers
  unit testing 73, 74
Spring Framework
  about 3
  and REST principles 3
Spring Web MVC
  URL 3
Subject Public Key Information (SPKI) 91

T

testing
  about 73
  load testing 83
  types 83
  User Acceptance Testing (UAT) 83
token-based authentication 64, 65
Tomcat instance 24
TRACE method 38
Trust on First Use security technique 91

U

Uniform Resource Identifiers (URIs) 2, 37
UNIX times
  URL 53
User Acceptance Testing (UAT) 83

V

Value-Object design pattern 29
versioning strategies
  about 33
  other approaches 35
  representation versioning 34
  URI versioning 33, 34

W

web services 1

X

XML-based communication protocol 1

Thank you for buying
Building a RESTful Web Service with Spring

About Packt Publishing

Packt, pronounced 'packed', published its first book, *Mastering phpMyAdmin for Effective MySQL Management*, in April 2004, and subsequently continued to specialize in publishing highly focused books on specific technologies and solutions.

Our books and publications share the experiences of your fellow IT professionals in adapting and customizing today's systems, applications, and frameworks. Our solution-based books give you the knowledge and power to customize the software and technologies you're using to get the job done. Packt books are more specific and less general than the IT books you have seen in the past. Our unique business model allows us to bring you more focused information, giving you more of what you need to know, and less of what you don't.

Packt is a modern yet unique publishing company that focuses on producing quality, cutting-edge books for communities of developers, administrators, and newbies alike. For more information, please visit our website at www.packtpub.com.

About Packt Open Source

In 2010, Packt launched two new brands, Packt Open Source and Packt Enterprise, in order to continue its focus on specialization. This book is part of the Packt Open Source brand, home to books published on software built around open source licenses, and offering information to anybody from advanced developers to budding web designers. The Open Source brand also runs Packt's Open Source Royalty Scheme, by which Packt gives a royalty to each open source project about whose software a book is sold.

Writing for Packt

We welcome all inquiries from people who are interested in authoring. Book proposals should be sent to author@packtpub.com. If your book idea is still at an early stage and you would like to discuss it first before writing a formal book proposal, then please contact us; one of our commissioning editors will get in touch with you.

We're not just looking for published authors; if you have strong technical skills but no writing experience, our experienced editors can help you develop a writing career, or simply get some additional reward for your expertise.

RESTful Java Patterns
and Best Practices

Learn best practices to efficiently build scalable, reliable,
and maintainable high performance RESTful services

Bhakti Mehta   PACKT open source

RESTful Java Patterns and Best Practices

ISBN: 978-1-78328-796-3   Paperback: 152 pages

Learn best practices to efficiently build scalable,
reliable, and maintainable high performance
RESTful services

1. Learn how to build RESTful services with
   JAX-RS 2.0.

2. Efficiently use the techniques outlined to build
   reliable and highly available applications based
   on REST.

3. Compare REST API from Twitter, GitHub,
   Facebook, and others in a conversational and
   easy-to-follow style.

Spring Security
Eugen Paraschiv

[PACKT] VIDEO

Spring Security [Video]

ISBN: 978-1-78216-865-2   Duration: 02:10 hours

An empirical approach to securing your web
applications

1. Fully secure your web application with
   Spring Security.

2. Implement authentication and registration with
   the database as well as with LDAP.

3. Utilize authorization examples that help
   guide you through the authentication of
   users step-by-step.

4. Learn with precise and practical examples
   for advanced security scenarios such as
   ACL, REST, and Remember Me.

Please check **www.PacktPub.com** for information on our titles

www.ingramcontent.com/pod-product-compliance
Lightning Source LLC
Chambersburg PA
CBHW060153060326
40690CB00018B/4100